They Make a Difference

T0194228

They Make a Difference

Men Say NO

Hada Sarhan

Order this book online at www.trafford.com
or email orders@trafford.com

Most Trafford titles are also available at major online book retailers.

© Copyright 2011 Hada Sarhan.
All rights reserved. No part of this publication may be reproduced, stored in a retrieval
system, or transmitted, in any form or by any means, electronic, mechanical, photocopying,
recording, or otherwise, without the written prior permission of the author.

Printed in the United States of America.

ISBN: 978-1-4269-6807-5 (sc)
ISBN: 978-1-4269-6808-2 (e)

Trafford rev. 05/04/2011

 www.trafford.com

North America & international
toll-free: 1 888 232 4444 (USA & Canada)
phone: 250 383 6864 ♦ fax: 812 355 4082

Also by Hada Sarhan

"Reem asks: who am I?".............. Arabic

"Women Say NO"...English

"When Men Flee"....................Arabic

Dedication

To my Husband, Love and Soul Mate Mohammad Kawash who believes that tough times do not last but tough people do.

Epigraph

"**I** learned that courage was not the absence of fear, but the triumph over it. The brave man is not he who does not feel afraid, but he who conquers that fear."

Nelson Mandela.

Contents

Introduction

Dr. Jamal Al Shalabi

The nine articles that make up this book offer an insight into the vital relationship between the media and culture; differently said, the articles selected purport to have the role today's media should in promoting cultures. Hada Sarhan's articles reflect the work she did amidst the socio-political developments storming the Middle East. And yet, apparently, most of the selected figures interviewed are westerners. Only two out of the eight articles presented in this book deal with Arab figures, namely: Abdul Bari Attwan, editor- in chief of the London- based Newspaper

Al-Quds Al-Arabi and Rashad abu Shawar, the accomplished Palestinian writer and man of letters. The rest of the articles are, in fact, interviews with western figures who hold contrasting, if not, antagonistic viewpoints vis-à-vis the policies and decisions of their countries, which are condemned by the Arab World, regarding the Palestinian issue and the situation in Iraqi.

The great significance of the viewpoints in the selected articles stems from the fact that they all emerged during times marked by sharp transitions in the Arab World, particularly the 2003 US occupation of Iraq and all the ensuing violence and destruction, as well as the bombings plaguing the whole Middle East and spreading to Europe, as seen in the Madrid bombings of 2004 and London bombings of 2005.

The goal of this book is neither to introduce unconventional viewpoints nor to present global or humane ones. Rather, it represents a crucial window through which the Arab reader could peer into the mind of others - be they European or American - through the eyes of outstanding writer Hada Sarhan. She wants to demonstrate that the West is not one or the same, and that the people of the Western world are not blindly following their leaders and regimes who wish to destroy the Islamic and Arab World with no reason, as the majority of Arabs believe.

There are voices to be heard, respected and nurtured because they are, above all, deeply humane. In this context, the author cites, for example, the Irish Denis Halliday, UN Humanitarian Coordinator, who "was driven to resignation" after a 34-year career with the UN over the economic sanctions imposed on Iraq, which he characterized as "genocide".

The author invested her journalistic knowledge to interview people who are/were either decision makers or somehow contributed to making decisions, by planning, drafting or commenting on decisions, employing for that their worldwide recognized journalistic, cultural and political clout.

Moreover, Sarhan conducted online interviews with American Larry E. Park, who served and bandaged wounds of many men, women and children during the Vietnam War of 1970 and 1971. While in service, Park realized the implications of the disastrous war and its impact on the future generations. This is what drove him to write an apology for his country's policies in Iraq. His interviewer asked him why he wrote the apology. He replied: "I become really ashamed and anguished when I watch TV or read reports on crimes against humanity in Iraq, crimes beyond the imagination ... I am sorry... I understand that." He continued: " American policies will be successful only when American tourists, workers, etc., can live and travel to Iraq and Afghanistan accompanied by no fear of death."

This book is the product of a five-year research project starting in 2004. It highlights the role of the media in advertising and promoting different attitudes and viewpoints. The word media here are not used in their traditional, narrow sense. Instead, they are extended to also include the book which holds artistic and cultural values.

I hope this book provides the readers, in general, westerners in particular, with an additional source of knowledge about understanding the other. It may enable readers to appreciate those who have good intentions and who are committed to maintaining a dialogue between the East and the West, between the Arab World and Europe, on the basis of mutual respect and understanding between civilizations and cultures. This is what the author attempts to demonstrate throughout this interesting and valuable book.

PREFACE

"They Make a Difference" is a selection of interviews conducts with men during my long journey in journalism in local, regional and international media in both Arabic and English languages. Some of these icons are: **Denis J. Halliday**, who resigned from his position as the United Nations Humanitarian Coordinator in Iraq after 34 years over the economic sanctions imposed on Iraq, describing them as "genocide", **Abdul Bari Attwan** writer and editor-in-chief of Al-Quds Al-Arabi, **Eliot Weinberger** essayist, translator and politician, **Rashad Abu Shawar** Palestinian novelist and rebellious storyteller, **Hans von Sponeck** who also served as a UN Humanitarian Coordinator for Iraq but resigned to protest UN's Iraq sanctions policy, **Richard Quest** CNN presenter, and **Stephen Farrell**, the Middle East Bureau Chief for "The Times of London," who was kidnapped in the Iraqi city of Fallujah in 2004, **Larry E. Park** a Vietnam Army medic who wrote his "apology" to the Iraqi people, and **Ben Wedeman** CNN's Cairo bureau chief has lived in the Middle East since 1974.

By Hada Sarhan

Denis J. Halliday

Denis J. Halliday was appointed the United Nations Humanitarian Coordinator in Iraq based in its New York Headquarters as the Assistant Secretary-General level from September 1997, until September 1998...

During this period, the Security Council Resolution 986 "Oil for Food" Programme, introduced in 1996/97 to assist the people of Iraq under the Economic Sanctions imposed by the Security Council.

Halliday, a national of Ireland, resigned from his position after 34 years with the UN over the economic sanctions imposed on Iraq, describing them as "genocide". He said: "We are in the process of destroying an entire society. It is as simple and terrifying as that. It is illegal and immoral."

Halliday holds an M.A. in Economics, Geography and Public Administration. He graduated from Trinity College, Dublin, Ireland and is married and has a daughter, Fransisca.

Your resignation is very courageous. What makes you take such a strong protest action?

- As the humanitarian coordinator at the time, I realized that the alleged concern for the welfare of the Iraqi people was nothing but a veil of pretention behind which major members of the UN Security Council planned their objective of regime replacement as a step towards consolidation of their power in the Middle East.

Some would say that to stay in office would help more the Iraqis?

- Had I seen a chance to make a difference for the human condition in Iraq under the circumstances in which the UN Security Council found itself at the time, I would have been prepared to stay on. There was no such chance as the Security Council was thoroughly dominated by the US and the UK using as major weapons of influence false information on weapons of mass destruction as well as on the state of human suffering despite UN efforts in Iraq to report conditions as they existed on the ground in Iraq.

In your book "Iraqi Autopsy" you describe the dreadful situations of the Iraqi people mainly the children, why do

you think the UN continues its policy of starvation of the innocent people of this country?

- UN Security Council policy was heavily influenced by the US and the UK governments. This policy initially used economic pressure as a tool to obtain political change. When this failed to materialize they shifted their emphasis from containment to regime change without concern for the people of Iraq. All 15 members of the Council were well aware of the evolving human catastrophe. The UN Security Council debates on Iraq give full testimony of this awareness. Most council members, however, did not have the political will let alone the moral integrity to make a difference against the heavy-handedness of the US and the UK governments and therefore share the burden of guilt.

Having served for thirty-six years with the UN organizations, what was your worst moment in your UN career?

- I joined the UN in 1968 as a young international civil servant believing in the ideals of the Charta. Thirty years later, in Baghdad in 1998, I saw firsthand that the ideals and the rhetoric of statesmen in support of these ideals quickly gave way when it did not suit the political, economic and strategic interests of those in a position of power. The realization that commitment was really no more than hypocrisy, that an Iraqi life was worth much less than a barrel of Iraqi oil and that facts had no weight to influence policy and that all of this translated into total helplessness of an international civil service was my worst moment in the United Nations. It was this moment that made me decide to resign from an institution in which I believed.

Though it was proved that Iraq had fulfilled the disarmament requirements of resolution 687 which demanded of Iraq the disarmament of all of its weapons of mass destruction

economic sanctions remained in place until the Anglo-American invasion of Iraq in March 2003?

- Economic sanctions remained in place until the illegal war of 2003 started because sanctions had little to do with freedom and liberation of a people. They had all to do with a determination to replace a dictator at whatever human cost for the sake of bilateral interests.

Do you agree that the positions taken by the United States in the Security Council during the 13 years of economic sanctions and military embargo against Iraq reveal that US Government concerns rested first with Iraq's weapons of mass destruction and US security interests?

- It is a fact, not even hidden by the US government that US Iraq policy evolved much more around weapons of mass destruction and US security interests than the welfare of a people. On 7 April 2004, Ambassador John D. Negroponte in a briefing for the Committee on Foreign Relations of the US Senate made no secret out of this when he said: "Although the flow of humanitarian and civilian goods to Iraq was a matter of strong interest to the US Government, it should be emphasized that an even greater preoccupation...was to ensure that no items were permitted for import which could in any way contribute to Iraq's WMD programs... We concentrated our efforts on this aspect of sanctions."

Why do you think despite the humanitarian programme socio-economic conditions in Iraq at the time sanctions were lifted in 2003 were so poor?

- The humanitarian exemption for Iraq was at no time ever remotely adequate to meet the needs of the Iraqi people. The financial allocations were knowingly inadequate; the bureaucratic nature of the import of essential humanitarian goods was horrendous and avoidable. The result was that at the end of the oil-for-food programme at the time when the illegal invasion started in March 2003, the allocation of humanitarian supplies on which the vast majority of Iraqis had to rely amounted to an average of $ 186 per person per year. This was the amount individual Iraqis had for food, medicines, water, electricity and sanitation, agriculture and education. It is commonly accepted that a person with less than one dollar per day lives in abject poverty. Iraqis during 61/2 years of the oil-for-food programme were forced to live with less than half of this amount. It cannot surprise that this reality allows the conclusion that economic sanctions on Iraq constitute another crime against humanity.

Do you think that the Security Council acts for the benefit of the international community not in the interest of individual member states?

- The UN Security Council has the responsibility to ensure that international policies are in the interest of the global community. Llyod Axworthy, Canada's foreign minister in the late 1990s reminded the Security Council of this responsibility when he said: "It is imperative that the sanctions reflect the objectives of the international community, not just the national interests of its most powerful members"!

The Security Council was unable to prevent the United States government to convert the Council into a tool box to be used in the pursuit of narrow US policy interests.

Was the Security Council aware that the introduction of two no-fly zones in Iraq by the US, UK and French governments was without international mandate and therefore illegal?

- The UN Security Council was fully aware that the southern and northern no-fly-zones originally established by the governments of the US, UK and France had no international legal basis and certainly no UN mandate. US and UK references to various UN resolutions, particularly resolution 688, often used by the US and UK to justify the maintenance of the no-fly zones, did not provide in any way legal cover. The no-fly zones were simply illegal. The dishonesty of US and UK intentions became increasingly clear after the 1998 Operation Desert Fox when US and UK pilots were given enlarged rules of engagement. This led to an increasing number of Iraqi civilian casualties as the UN reported from Baghdad in 1999/2000. For this the UN was reprimanded by the US and the UK and eventually forced to stop air strike reporting. As the March 2003 date for the illegal US/UK invasion came closer, the two governments used the two no-fly zones to prepare for war by destroying military installations. The real objective of the maintenance of the two no fly-zones was not to protect ethnic and religeous groups but in   destabilizing the country.

Do you think that the reports sent by the investigators of mass destruct ions helped the US governments to invade Iraq?

- The reports of UNMOVIC in late 2002/early 2003 were anything but helpful to the US as they showed that there were no traces of WMD as alleged by Secretary of State Colin Powell in his dishonest presentation to the UN Security Council on 5 February nor did Dr. Blix and his colleagues support the US contention that the Government of Iraq was uncooperative and therefore in 'material breach' justifying 'serious consequences' according to UN resolution 1441. The high costs of maintaining US and British troops in the Gulf, the deteriorating morale of the waiting troops, the soaring temperatures and an increasingly critical public back home and internationally combined with an

unstoppable determination by the Bush administration to invade
Iraq explain the start of the March 2003 war.

**Was there any kind of corruption in the oil-for-food-program?
And were there any "big" names involved?**

- The Third Volcker Commission report on the oil-for-food
programme has just been issued and suggests that there has been
individual wrongdoing. It is important to point out that there is
no evidence that there is an institutional base of corruption but a
limited though serious misuse of privileged position by a few.

**Do you think there is a connection between invading Iraq and
the worldwide spread of violence and terrorism? And do you
think invading Iraq was a must for the US security, though
no connections were found between Al QED and Iraq?**

- As the recent Iraq Tribunal in Istanbul has shown, there is a worldwide anger against the US and the UK because of the illegal war
against Iraq preceded by 13 years of devastating economic sanctions.
This anger has unfortunately encouraged extreme elements to carry
out acts of crime. A global public majority demands of political
leaders that they address the causes of extremism as a first significant
step towards reducing extremism and acts of crime. If leaders in the
US and UK do not understand this demand they will continue to add
to their liability for what must be expected as further deteriorating
global security circumstances in the period ahead.

Abdul Bari Attwan

When you walk down King's Road in the British capital, where the stores and restaurants are spread all over and the king's path is bustling with activity and liveliness in spite of the economic recession, your mind won't even imagine that the Arab press offices you are looking for are hidden behind this London frontage.

And when you enter through that old door and cross into *Al-Quds Al-Arabi newspaper, you will not believe that this voice, which reaches remote locations in this world, originates here, from this limited space that is so deceptive upon* the first impression. This is where you learn how modest the scene is compared to the scenes created by the lavish amounts of money that other migratory papers spend on their offices and correspondents.

However, Abdul Bari Attwan, editor-in-chief, finds this modesty to be a unique feature in favor of *Al-Quds Al-Arabi, which carries some of his peevish characters and* cantankerous nature. Arab audience always anticipate his appearance on satellite television whenever an accident or a war begins in the region, especially because of everything he is known for, such as his sharp positions and his overt, heaping accusations that are destitute of any courtesy.

In this narrow space occupied by a widely distributed Arabic newspaper, Abdul Bari Attwan welcomed us ... and said while he was smiling, "I welcome you into this modest office, rejecting the advice that Mohamed Dahlan gave me when he visited me once upon a time and told me, 'Your prestige outside is so notorious, and I advise you to avoid receiving anyone in your newspaper. Let your prestige be big. This office reduces your prestige.' Yet, my prestige is from this place."

I asked Abdul Bari Attwan some questions about his life journey, his position, confrontations, and life stopovers, and, below, we have provided both the queries and the answers he gave:

Why did you choose expatriate (émigré) journalism, and does your presence in London give you a wider margin of freedom? What are the obstacles that face expatriate journalism or journalism in exile?

I thank you, because you are the first person to say that my presence in London has given me a wider margin of freedom. They always say that you are staying in London as though I have a castle or a feudal estate in the Arab homeland that I abandoned or a passport that I relinquished and came to London. They have overdone it.

I wonder how I can return to Gaza, for neither the Egyptians nor the Israelis would allow me.

In London, there is something basic that is called the law. In this country, there is a state that is a state of law, and as long as you adhere to the law, none will bother you or infringe on your rights.

For example, the Saudi government threatened to cancel the Yamama deal worth $80 billion if the British government does not intervene or hand over the Saudi opposition figure Muhammad Al-Masari, and it did not succeed in doing so. Major and Blair tried to explain that this could not be done except by legal means. The independence of the courts here protects us.

In London, it is impermissible to withdraw my passport, to arrest or torture me, or to prevent me from entering into the country or leaving it, such as is the case in the Arab countries, where I do not have a passport but documents. I acquired the British passport to be able to move like human beings, which gave me freedom, confidence, and capability. Here in London, I am protected by the law.

There are harassments, which I printed in my book *"A Country of Words"*, such as the Madrid bombings, where I received a statement from al-Qaeda in which it claimed responsibility. I published the statement, and if I were reticent, the Socialist government would not have come to power nor would Aznar, the ally of Blair and Bush, have remained. At the time, the British government seized my computer … but legally.

I suffer from harassments from Arab countries, some of which exercised their influence by closing *Al-Quds Al-Arabi*, and they even applied pressures on British television so as not to host me, because according to them, I am a supporter of terrorism, and they tried to prevent me from appearing on the BBC.

Some Arab countries tried to prevent the printing of *Al-Quds Al-Arabi* whereupon we submitted a request in Morocco. And at the last moment, Saudi Arabia intervened, and the decision was revoked. We were also prevented from printing in the Dubai free zone.

We are surprised by the extent of harassment that we face, and whenever we speak to the press, the Mosad takes extracts and posts them on YouTube, characterizing me as a terrorist.

A Lebanese station asked me, "What would be your feeling if Iran strikes Israel?" I said that I would come out and dance. They posted this on YouTube and described me as a terrorist who wishes to destroy Israel with nuclear weapons.

Many wait for your appearance on television screens in times of crisis. Why are you always tense? And have you thought of owning a satellite television station or moving from print journalism to the visual media?

I am the son of a refugee camp. My father died, and I bore responsibility for ten brothers at an early age. I worked in a tomato factory in Marka and was a garbage collection truck driver at Amman Municipality, and I worked on a sprinkler tractor and was a sweets distributor for Nashed Ikhwan. My origins are the street, from the bottom of society. If I do not have concern for the issues and feelings of people and if I do not sympathize with them, then with whom should I empathize, with the bourgeoisie?

They hold it against me that I am very emotional! Why not? Am I not human? Do I not witness the murder of children and destruction?

Regarding *Al-Quds Al-Arabi*, I have received many offers, and I take pride that Al Jazeera based its style, success, and experience on *Al Quds Al-Arabi*. I received an offer through a person in the amount of $150 million to convert *Al Quds Al-Arabi* experience into a satellite TV station.

I do not need fame. What would I do with it, for I am neither an actor nor a signer to enjoy fame? My financial situation is okay, and I have what is enough for me. And my children have received an education and have graduated and are working presently. I have twenty years of work in the newspaper, so what would a satellite TV station do for me?

My ambition is to relieve myself of responsibility at the newspaper. Actually, I am lucky for having a working team that has not changed for twenty years, and we have no secrets at the newspaper. And we take pride that our experience in the world of journalism is unique.

At the outset, you wished for *Al-Quds Al-Arabi* to be a newspaper that is concerned with cultural affairs, and you declared excluding the rhyming column poetry. My question is this: Why such exclusion?

Those poets drove me mad, for those poets are of diverse groups and orientations. May God rest the soul of my friend Mahmoud Darwish who used to characterize them as the five-minute alliances.

When we founded *Al-Quds Al-Arabi*, my ambition was to focus more on the cultural section, because when we started in 1989, when there was a sort of Arab solidarity and harmony, and it is known that the press cannot survive in the shadow of conciliation, especially in our Arab countries and the Third World, for we are used to battles, differences, and clashes. The Arabs used to be in harmony, and there were no camps. As an editor-in-chief, I wish for the newspaper to succeed. Amjad Nasser, who is a poet and a friend of mine, is no doubt a modernist who has a good vision. We sat at one of the train stations, planning and thinking about the new project.

My relationship to culture and poetry specifically is not strong, and I sufficed myself by a love letter to the neighbor's daughter, which I wrote when I was young. She did not like it, and since then, I gave up poetry.

Amjad was a partisan of free verse and against rhyming poetry, and they held a position toward him. And like opposing Jews, they opposed the rhyming poem, and I did not interfere in their method and style, given that I trust them. Even though I grew up on the poetry of Mutanabbi and the poetry meters, I felt that the youth are zealous, for I am with change, and the outcome was more enemies.

You said that *Al-Quds Al-Arabi* is indebted to the martyr Saddam Hussein and Osama Bin Laden. Could you explain this to us?

There is no person more intentionally misunderstood in this Arab cultural life than Abdel Bari Attwan, because there are people who intentionally take my words out of context.

In 1990, after the invasion of Kuwait, we were among the few Arab newspapers that stood against the American project. All the gulf was against us, States who have money and media.

Egypt, with its splendid media and history, stood against us ... and also Syria, with its revolutionary history and nationalist tradition, stood against us. It was a terrible alliance—an alliance of money from the gulf states and Saudi Arabia, a giant state economically alongside its Islamic influence.

We were actually a newspaper still in its beginnings. We were poor and destitute. We were in a miserable condition and in a desperate situation, and the front that was with us was in a desperate situation—weak, without money or influence or media. This is why we were abused … and facts were hidden from us.

If I were an opportunist, I would have gone to those states, and if I wanted to be comfortable like others, I would have joined the fold of those countries. And I would not have had this modest office that you see, and I would have had ten cars and security guards.

As for the matter of Saddam and Bin Laden, I had an interview with Rotana TV about my life after the publication of my book *"A Country of Words"*. At the time, I said facetiously, "It is a coincidence that there are two people to whom I am indebted for the success of *Al-Quds* newspaper, and I do not mean that they gave me money or that I supported Bin Laden." What I meant was that in 1990, we were a small newspaper by contrast to empires, such as *Al Hayat* and *Al Sharq Al Awsat* when the invasion of Kuwait took place, and we stood against the American project because our compass necessities for us to stand always against America and Israel, whereupon our newspaper, with a distribution of a thousand copies or two thousand copies, for example, increased by 2,000 percent, because we represented another perspective. And so people favored us, and thus I said, "Thanks to Saddam Hussein, because his invasion to Kuwait helped the newspaper to succeed."

As for the story of Osama Bin Laden, after my interview with him, which played a great role in my life, moving me from a local Arab journalist to an international journalist, and thereafter the September 11th events, and so there were forty television cameras awaiting me in front of the newspaper. I also published a book on al-Qaeda that was printed thrice in Britain only and was translated into twenty languages read around the world.

This is what I mean by saying they played a role in my life. The first increased the circulation of the newspaper, and Bin Laden moved me to an international dimension and made me publish books. But the tendentious people focused only on those two lines in an interview that lasted for two hours.

Has any state proposed to you to settle in it?

A: I wish I could go to any Arab country, but I want an independent judiciary. Give me an independent judiciary, and I would go tomorrow. It is unacceptable to have a corrupt judiciary, corrupt regimes, repressive dictatorships and intelligence services that govern. How could I feel comfortable when I know that they will arrest me or seize my passport or prevent me from travelling? How I wish for our newspaper to be printed in an Arab country. But we are fought every day, and our websites are hacked. However, I will say to the credit of Jordan that our website has not been prohibited for fifteen years. The credit is due to King Hussein. (God rest his soul.) When the press and publications department banned us, he intervened personally and said that henceforth no newspaper would be banned or shut down.

How would you describe the Palestinian arena now, and is there a hope for overcoming the existing division? Or are there two opposing and irreconcilable orientations?

In my view, we are witnessing in the Palestinian arena the end of a phase and the beginning of a new one. The Palestinian arena is perennially capable of self-renewal like everything else.

During the days of Ahmad Al-Shuqairi in 1964, the Palestine Liberation Organization had characteristics that were suited for the Arab circumstance at the time, where the official Arab regimes desired Palestinian organizations with an army. The impression was that the armies alone were capable of liberating Palestine rather than the resistance.

But with the change of the concept after the Battle of Karamah and the appearance of resistance movements, the concept of a classic army that would liberate Palestine was eroded and receded against the backdrop of guerilla activity. It was natural then for the skin and heart of the PLO to change.

Al-Shuqairi was removed and replaced by Hammoudeh in 1969 and then by Yasser Arafat as head of the organization, which came to rely on resistance and not on the classic armies. The reliance in the quest for liberation moved from the regimes to the resistance movements—that is, the Palestinian would take the initiative himself.

The Palestinian scene has changed now, and the Fateh movement has chosen the path of negotiations and peaceful resolution. And there is the belief that peaceful resolution is better and that resistance is an inappropriate option, as Abbass stated on more than one occasion, describing the martyrdom operations as mean, and that rocket attacks are futile and that the peace option is the sole course of action.

Presently, the peace option has failed in the wake of the Israeli elections and the triumph of the right, where the rightists were competing against the rightists. Practically, the picture changed, and the peace process collapsed. And it became impossible to achieve peace with Lieberman or with a coalition government that included extremists, for instance.

Practically speaking, the peace option is over. Presently, Abbas should review all his history. He either reverts to resistance or bids you farewell, for his project has failed.

In the past, the pressure was on Hamas and the resistance movements. Presently, it must join the authority or decrease its extremism and become moderate and enlist in the Palestinian political project, which is based on reconciliation. Now, this option is not available. On the contrary, it is incumbent on the authority and its remnants to revert to the Hamas grounds and not the opposite. The arena now is on the threshold of an old choice, and the old forms have fallen. The peace process has fallen, and the chief negotiators have fallen. No negotiations. Either they rely on resistance or leave the arena for those who wish to resist.

Is Oslo over, and are you optimistic for the future?

I have always been critical of it, and I differed with Arafat after the signing of Oslo. I was very close to him with respect and without being dependent. There were differences between us, and when he signed Oslo, I told him that he would not succeed, that they would not give him anything and that they would use him. He offered me a ministerial position in the authority through his representative, Jibril Rjoub. I declined the offer after being made the offer personally. I declined the offer because I was not convinced of that project. Presently, the picture has changed as proven by the fact that Yasser Arafat himself stopped believing in Oslo.

I remember when we parted. But the relationship remained fictitious, and there were polite differences between us. Even though I criticized him vehemently and I was harsh on him, he tolerated me.

On one occasion, he held my hand, and we walked in the street, because he was concerned about eavesdropping in his offices. He said to me, "I know that you are against Oslo and rightly so, but I wish to tell you something that I will ask you not to write about except after my death. You will see the Israelis fleeing Palestine, and their project has started ending."

Thus, when I used to be harsh on him, he used to say, "Oh, Abdel Bari, I adhere to my commitment. Do you understand me?"

I would say, "Yes, I understand you."

I take pride in one thing, namely that I contributed to rendering a failure the Camp David negotiations ... or I helped Arafat to make them a failure when they applied pressure on him to make concessions. Arafat used the break and requested Abu Mazen to disclose that the pressure on Arafat were from inside the delegation..

They forbade the participants to use mobile phones or to avail communications, but Abu Mazen left to attend his son's wedding in London and sent me a letter stating that those exerting pressure on Arafat were from inside the delegation. And I printed this, which was one of the reasons for reducing the pressure on Arafat. Practically speaking, I am optimistic, because I have confidence in the ability of the people and the Arab nation. I was never prejudiced based on national origin, and I take pride in having friends in Jordan, including Abdel Karim Al-Dughmi, Mamdouh Abbadi, Khaled Mhadin, Fares Nabulsi, and Mahmoud Al-Kayed. I am an Arab nationalist with deep Islamic roots, and I have faith and confidence in the nation. We will triumph. The Israeli project will not succeed because it is racist and sectarian. This was evidenced in the elections where the extremists, who are actually against peace and against coexistence, won.

What about the Iraqi scene?

The Iraqi scene has given me complexes. It has perplexed and shocked me. When Iraq entered Kuwait, we were not with the invasion, and I actually wrote an editorial in which I said that the action was a mistake. But when half a million American soldiers came, the smallest Palestinian child realizes that it is implausible for the Americans to come to serve the nation and Kuwait. Rather, there was a project, and I wrote that we loved Kuwait but also loved Iraq.

Wherever the American trench, we are in the opposing trench. Presently, we are defending Iran and its right to have a nuclear program.

We supported Hezbollah, and we were not sectarian, contrary to some Iraqis who believed that we support Saddam because he is a Sunni.

What shocked me concerning Iraq was the extent of sectarianism in that secular state, which used to be a model for coexistence between people. I was shocked by the extent of sectarian hatred and its exploitation by some quarters. What shocked me more was that people turned into a tool of the American project against their country. I am in London, and I see them with their families in Britain. They used to live on social security, and they have become billionaires. Those people used to speak about corruption in the Saddam era and about the sons and daughters of Saddam, and now look at them. I was shocked when Al Arabiyyah wanted to blemish Saddam and to show him at the birthday parties of his daughter, Hala. Actually, there are ordinary people who celebrate in a grander and more conspicuous manner.

Look at the cars of their sons, their properties, and houses in London.

And just as Afghanistan was behind the collapse of the Soviet Union, Iraq is the beginning of the collapse of the American empire. It is no coincidence that the president is asking for $700 billion from congress in order to save the economy. This is the size of its loss in Iraq. What made him lose such an amount? It is the heroic Iraqi resistance.

What also shocked me was that some people who used to fight with al-Qaeda were ready to blow themselves up with al-Qaeda and with the Iraqi resistance and also be bought by America for $300, and they are eight hundred thousand ... to fight against the resistance, which fights for their country. You don't want al-Qaeda. We can understand! But to fight the Iraqi resistance, this is something that we can't understand or fathom.

Then there are those who shed tears for Iraq and Iraqi independence. But didn't you know that Iran is strengthening its influence in Iraq? Nature is averse to a vacuum, and when there was a vacuum in Iraq, it was filled by Iran.

The forces that entered Iraq moved from an Arab territory. You destroy Iraq, and then you say that Iran took it over!

I am still a believer in the Arabism of Iraq and in the Iraqi individual who is heroic, innovative, and has seven thousand years of civilization behind him. I believe that this is a temporary phase that entails negative aspects and that the Iraqi people will overcome this phase.

I take pride that Saddam sent representatives thrice and offered funding, but I did not want to take the side of Saddam because of a source of funding. Muzaffar Amin, the last Iraqi ambassador in London, presently in Amman, approached me to offer funding, and I rejected his offer, because my position in support of Iraq is ethical. I am prideful that before Saddam was executed and martyred, his lawyer came to me, and I was the last to see him. He told me, "I have a trust from Saddam that I wanted to give you." He also said that the president sat three hours and tasked him with contacting

Attwan and to tell him that Saddam was proud of him and thanked him for all his positions. "You are a true Arab, and a nation with Attwan is undefeatable." When he was leaving, he told him not to forget to convey this message.

For me, this is worth the entire world. They lashed me because of my position. I stood by the Arabism and honor of Iraq, which is the honor of the Arab nation.

Presently, they say that Iran is a danger to the Arab nation, but was it not the martyr Saddam who created equilibrium (balance) in the Arab region? Are not those who complain of Iranian encroachment the ones who have destroyed Iraq and who have disturbed the historical and strategic balance?

Is there real change in the Arab situation regarding the Palestine and Arab issues, or is what happened merely a change of the color of the president in the White House?

Let us admit first of all that democracy has allowed the son of an African Muslim immigrant to become president of the greatest country on earth. This cannot happen in an Arab state, except through a coup d'état, not through natural and democratic means, because there is no democracy! Had Obama been born in an Arab state, he wouldn't have had a passport and would have remained a slave.

Unfortunately, we are racist and have too many racists among us. The regime, which allowed an individual to develop, to get his doctorate from Harvard, and to run the legal publication of Harvard's law school, has become president because he worked through the system and because the system was ready for him to become president. That is, a historical moment had dawned, one that allowed a black man to become president because America got itself involved in two wars (Iraq and Afghanistan), failed, and lost them both. Fortunately, when the Republican candidate began to really compete, the economy collapsed. The outcome of botched military adventures unfolded full-blown before taxpayers. After all, the West only understands the language of the "pocketbook."

A British person, and I speak from thirty years of experience, only understands what enters into his bank account at the end of the month. He cares little about pride, dignity, and valor, for these are secondary and marginal issues to him. The main thing is what he stands to gain or lose. When the economic crisis transpired, the people demanded change. That was the moment that made Obama's presence possible. If he made it, we'd say the system made him. If he failed, we'd say it was because he's black.

What about Obama's position on the Middle East?

Most black people are like Arabs and stand against the white man colonialism that humiliated him … and transformed him into Uncle Tom. Obama knew that Iraq was a failed adventure, and he would not achieve any victory in Afghanistan. But he knew that he was working within institutional framework that was ruled by well-established organizations, not individuals.

I had a strange story about something that happened with me during the Iraqi War in 2003.

I had once said in a speech at a university that Blair implicated Britain in a war, jeopardized its interests in the Middle East, and exposed it to danger, for it could have been targeted by al-Qaeda. After finishing, I met with the president of that university, and he said to me, "I liked what you said and the passion that filled your speech, but you should know that whoever was the prime minister of Britain at the time was going to follow the same course of action like Blair, whether he was from the Conservative or the Labor Party. That is because we are the ones who make the decisions. We make policy, and the prime minister has to follow. We, as an institution, made a mistake in 1956 by invading the Suez without coordination with America and without its approval. As a result, we paid a hefty price and lost our empire. Since then, we have decided to side with America no matter what, right or wrong. Convinced or not, we have decided to stand with America, and we know our decisions in that regard may not always be the right ones."

America just like Britain is ruled by an institution. In the senate, there's an arms lobby, an oil lobby, a universities lobby, etc., all of which form the ruling institution. This institution won't let Obama make decisions all by himself. He has to observe the institution, of course. Thus, we have to learn a lot. We have to admit that America led a black man to the presidency as proof that democracy is the best form of government.

What about Obama's stance on Iraq?

Obama realizes that America's economic loss and the war in Iraq had a lot to do with the economic crisis. America has lost $700 billion so far in Iraq, and the meter is still running. Obama realized that the American presence in Iraq was a loss. And he knows that time changes things. For example, the American situation in Iraq is getting better right now. The elections took place. The security situation has gotten better because the Americans have bribed some Iraqi forces and created Al Sahwah (the Awakening). They established security checkpoints and divided up Baghdad with Babylonian walls. They cultivated sectarian divisions and increased American forces by twenty thousand. They achieved a great deal of success. But will that last? Obama realizes such success may not last, as it happened in Afghanistan in October 2002 when Taliban and al-Qaeda were totally destroyed, and now after seven years, Taliban and al-Qaeda are back and are occupying 80 percent of Afghanistan. This can happen anywhere, with al-Qaeda and others coming back. Obama realizes this is a losing battle and that he must pull out American forces and extricate himself of that situation. Why should he continue to lose? And this is regarding Iraq. On Afghanistan, it's a big mistake. He thinks that troop increases in Afghanistan will solve the problem. Unfortunately, he is not a good reader of history. I have written a book on Afghanistan.

I know that the tribes that are opposed to the Pishtun are with Karzai, and they did not do anything. Moreover, the Afghan people, and especially the Pishtun tribes, which are the largest, and the Taliban is with them, and they have a principle that states that whoever takes refuge with their tribe is safe, even if he is a killer. The most shameful thing to them is to hand over a person. Hence, they cannot do anything against al-Qaeda like they did in Iraq. Al-Qaeda committed immense mistakes in Iraq, such as considering people to be apostates and the amputation of a thief's hand. But in Afghanistan, it is not possible to expel al-Qaeda, for they fought with them for the sake of their country, and Mulla Umar refused to hand over Bin Laden to the Americans or Saudis, because he sought asylum and they cannot violate this principle.

Moreover, only 5 percent of the Afghani people are educated, for it is a very primitive region and the nation is extremist in totality, and the Afghanis subscribe to the Hanafi Islamic school of law, which is more dangerous than the Wahhabi school.

And the success of Obama in Afghanistan is almost, if not totally, impossible.

And to revert to the Palestine issue, Obama has disappointed us and me personally, for in the Gaza carnage, he did not show sympathy—he who is black and who has come from the lowest levels of American society—and his father's name is Hussein. The entire world, even the cold-blooded British, showed sympathy and condemned the massacres and took a position, while he was like the sphinx. He compares his black children with the children of Israel. Why does he not liken them to the children of Palestine? Nevertheless, it is difficult at present to judge.

Regarding Iraq, there are some tendentious people who say that if America should withdraw from Iraq, there would be a sectarian war, and the beneficiary of such a view is the beneficiary of occupation. The Islamic Party in Iraq is a partisan of the reconciliation front inside parliament, and those are beneficiaries of the occupation, for without the latter, they would not exist and it would have been impossible for them to be deputies. And the Iraqi people would have brought them to justice, for the occupation favored them and created for them the Green Zone. And they are a state within a state, and they know full well that should the American forces withdraw from Iraq, the project would collapse or would be exposed to disintegration and that they would lose the umbrella of American protection. They threatened Al-Maliki to sign for security measures, and thereafter, they acquiesced because they became threatened. And most of them do not support American withdrawal. One hundred and forty-five thousand American soldiers protect them on the pretext that they protect Iraq and the Green Zone. And now, five to six years since the occupation, the Baghdad airport road is not safe, and foreign presidents make sudden visits without prior notice. And we were surprised by the visits of Sarkozy and Bush to the Green Zone.

The withdrawal will take place not out of a keenness for the independence of Iraq but to serve American interests—an America that is not able to bear the losses arising from its presence in Iraq.

Given your latest book, *"A Country of Words"* , your CV and career, there are many readers who do not know who

Abdel Bari Attwan is, where he comes from, why he chose the journalistic profession, and why this timing. Also, what comes after *"A Country of Words"*?

My hobby is not to author and publish books. I believe that a CNN interview watched by five hundred million viewers is better than writing a book. My first book, *Al-Qaeda*, discusses the secret history of al-Qaeda. When I lectured at universities, students and professors would approach me and ask whether I had books. All who wrote about al-Qaeda were foreign authors, and I was the first Arab Muslim to write about al-Qaeda.

They held dialogues with me about al-Qaeda and recorded them, so I thought; *Why not write a book about al-Qaeda?* And I was surprised and flabbergasted by the extraordinary success, for in a year and a half, the book was printed six times by a British company, and those companies have credibility. The book was translated into twenty languages and was printed in America three times, and in Australia, it is a best seller. And it is available in a majority of universities in the world, and it is a basic reference.

Three hundred thousand copies were sold, and every year, it is translated to other language. And incidentally, there has been a printing of the book in Portugal and Brazil.

My life is multicolored and has events and adventures, and it has not been an easy life—from a refugee camp to London. I was driven to write a chapter on Palestine but in a different and human style, with all its comical and tragic dimensions, and I presented the refugee camp in a different manner, one in which all are equal, even the romantic relationships. And I talked about my trip to Jordan and my working at a tomato factory where the leaders of the resistance held political meetings. I also talked about Egypt and the turbulent period preceding the October war and Sadat. I wrote also about personal experiences and talked about

Jordan and the Battle of Karameh, circumcision, the open Europe, and the difficulties involved in the process of acclimatization to European society.

I spoke about my Arab Palestinian wife from Kuwait and the story of meeting her. I spoke about Yasser Arafat and numerous human aspects, and I devoted a full chapter to the right of return. And I started it when I returned to Palestine for the first time in forty years and saw the country.

Eliot Weinberger

An essayist, translator, editor and politician, Eliot Weinberger's books include Works on Paper, Outside Stories, Written Reaction, Karmic Traces, The Stars, and the forthcoming Muhammad. His work has been published in some thirty languages.

Weinberger's Political articles are collected in "What I Heard About Iraq, and What Happened Here" and was awarded the National Book Critics Circle award for criticism and selected for the Times Literary Supplement's "International Books of the Year."

Weinberger is widely recognized as one of America's leading translators of Latin American poetry. He is the editor of the anthologies American Poetry Since 1950: Innovators & Outsiders and World Beat: International Poetry Now from New Directions.

In 1992, he was the first recipient of the PEN/Kolovakos Award for his promotion of Hispanic literature in the U.S.; and became the only American literary writer to be awarded the Order of the Aztec Eagle by the government of Mexico. He is a curator of the Berlin International Literature Festival, Weinberger lives in New York City.

As essayist, translator, and editor, do you feel that writers are under siege?

Writers are always under siege in countries where the government is afraid of dialogue, or of new ideas. And certainly there are places today where writers are being censored, exiled, imprisoned, or executed. But I do not think that, globally, the situation is now worse than it has been for the last 100 years. And, with the internet– a means of communication that is very difficult for a state to control– it may well be a little better.

Do you think that the poetry has changed forever after September 11th? If yes in what way and what do you think poet should do?

Poetry hasn't changed at all after September 11. In fact, very little poetry written in the USA is concerned with the larger realities of being alive in Bush America. It is a kind of a scandal. This is partially because the USA is the only nation on earth where poets and fiction writers are not public intellectuals. They have no access to the newspapers or television or radio, and rarely comment on social or political issues

To what extend does this tragic (September 11th) affected your poems?

Since the inauguration of Bush in January 2001, I have been writing articles on what is going in the USA for publication abroad, in order to demonstrate, at the least, that the USA is not a monolith of opinion. (This has now become more obvious– with Bush's popularity polls at 31%– than it was not so long ago.) My writing as a poet has informed some of these articles– particularly in "What I Heard About Iraq," a kind of documentary prose poem– more than political events have informed my more literary writings.

You've argued that the shortage of translation activity among contemporary U.S. poets reflects a generalized poverty of cultural perspective and imagination. And that 'most of the great ages of literature have been great ages of translation,' Is there reason to think the radically new and unfolding international context might have a stimulating effect on the practice and status of literary translation?

Although the USA is a nation of immigrants, it is strangely insular and ignorant of most of the world. 20% of high school students cannot find the USA on a world map. Of the 180,000 books published here every year, about 250-300 are translations of foreign literature. This, however, is beginning to change. One of the spurs to translation is a general disgust with one's own culture– one becomes eager for other perspectives, other ideas. In recent years, the kind of people who read and write literature have become very unhappy with the USA, and are sick of the demonization of other cultures. For the first time since the 1960's– a similar period in our history– we are eager to hear from people who are not us. It is a strange paradox, but Bush has been very good for translation!

once you said :"it seems to me that the next great age, one that has already begun, belongs to writers in the major European languages who are not white.." what makes you think that?

A national literature depends on new forms of expression to remain vibrant, and one of the best sources, besides translation, is new people speaking the language. It is safe to say that, speaking in general terms; the most interesting writers today in French come from, or live in, the Francophone areas of Africa and the Caribbean. In English, the liveliest new fiction writers are from the Indian Diaspora. In Europe, the current anti-immigrant hysteria is preoccupied with the idea of "preserving our culture." What they do not realize is that the immigrants are in fact keeping their culture alive. Decadence is the same old people repeating the same old things to themselves.

Are you familiar with Arabs literary works?

Sadly, very little contemporary Arab literature is translated. I read the poets and novelists who are, and in recent years I have been reading the classical poets, historians like al-Tabari and al-Masudi, selections from the Hadith, and various philosophers. I have written a very short literary book about Muhammad– also a kind of documentary prose poem– which will be published in September. I retell some of the stories about him that are familiar to Muslims but unknown to the rest of the world, in the attempt to convey some of the wonder that surrounds this complex and fascinating sacred and historical figure. It is my little gesture against the anti-Muslim sentiment in so much of the West.

Four years have passed since the invasion of Iraq but with no progress, on the contrary, the situation is getting worse. Why do you think the main planners and advisers behind the war in Iraq get it so wrong?

Cheney and Rumsfeld and the others – Bush is merely their spokesman, and is not involved in the actual running of the government– really believed that they could march into Iraq, overthrow Saddam, and easily install a puppet government that would give them permanent military bases and unlimited access to the oil. Overthrowing the Saddam regime, which was collapsing anyway, was easy. As they knew nothing about the country, it never occurred to them the end of Saddam would unleash complex rival factions, or that the people in general might not be so happy about a foreign invader declaring them now to be "free."

In your opinion how could one guarantee an objective and an* inaccurate history for the coming generation?

The history of the Iraq war and of the Bush administration is just beginning to be written. Many facts are just beginning to be revealed. Many people believe that history will judge this as, by far, the worst American presidency of modern times.

Richard Quest

Future Space Travel

Well known CNN presenter Richard Quest, 44, dreams of experiencing the sense of leaving planet earth behind and looking down on it from space, even if only for a brief time. Quest, a British born presenter who works for CNN International, anchoring "Business International" from London plus two monthly programs, "Business Traveller" and "Quest" advices promising journalists to develop their own personal style and count themselves lucky to have joined this fabulous profession that enables us to witness the events that shape our world from the very frontline. Quest studied Law at the University of Leeds, in1985, and then joined CNN in 2001 for the launch of "Business

International". Since this time Quest has covered a variety of different events for CNN.

How well do you know Jordan?

The answer is, not well enough. In the early days of the question show I was very fortunate to go to Jordan. We attended the Nobel Laureate summit at Petra. What an extraordinary evening to listen to the orchestra playing, having dinner amongst such extraordinary sights and amongst wonderful company. I assure you; that's not something you forget in a hurry. Petra was an amazing setting for this meeting of great minds and I absolutely loved that trip. It wetted my appetite to return

Are you familiar with Jordanian or Arab media? What is your evaluation of the journalistic standards in this part of the world?

Whichever way you look at it journalism in the Middle East is becoming increasingly lively. There is more and more choice….. that that can only be a good thing. With choice comes diversity and with diversity comes journalism to be proud of. Everyone won't like everything, but I know the feeling… not everyone likes me!

Do you think that journalists are still being submissive to authorities?

It is the nature of journalists to question authority and those in power. That is the very raison d'etre of serious journalism. And the reverse of that coin is that power tries to influence our reporting. This happens to some degree in all societies. Unfortunately it can reach the point where the restrictions are so severe that there is no choice but to submit. As an international channel, at CNN we do not operate under any one direct governmental influence and yet we are often regulated by many of the countries where we broadcast. In the end, all you can do is report the facts clearly, accurately and with no bias. You do the best job you can….and never forget, the audience can see quite clearly if you are trying to tell them black is white or similar.

You said also that the worst form of censorship is self-censorship, don't you think that such censorship may hinder you from doing your job?

Exactly; that's why I said it! Obviously by definition we all self-censor in some way as you have to respect the limits of the law and the limits of decency in broadcasting! What I was referring to was the self-censorship that comes about because of what you know will be allowed by external censors or governments. Especially in the field of political or business reports. Self-censorship in dark, smoky rooms is the enemy of good journalism.

You once said: when you enter this profession you must leave your opinions with your hat and your coat on the door. Do you think a journalist could do this?

Let's clear something up straight away. Absolute objectivity is not possible, nor is it desirable. When you broadcast you are informing and entertaining. But being passionate about telling a story does not mean you are biased. You go out to do a story with an open mind on what you might find. There might be very good reasons why a government has done something – they deserve to be put in the story as well. I have learned from bitter experience that these things are never one sided and only a poor journalist closes their mind to the other side. Let's leave it to the wisdom of the viewer to decide which side they prefer.

As for my own reporting, in all the newsrooms I have worked in, strong editors supervising my reporting have been able to temper my excesses or question my reporting. Why did you say that? What's the evidence for that statement? Are you sure about that fact? Who told you that? Is this article biased? None of us are so senior or experienced that we don't need a second pair of eyes to question our assessments. Also none of us should be allowed to report on matters where we have a clear, vested interest. And that means more than just financial reporting.

Do you feel that television makes news look frivolous?

That is a very old and tired argument. And they said that the Wireless would kill the written word. Oh, yes, and the written word would be sure to be end of society! The predictions of how dire television can be go right back to the 1950s. Read Newton Minow's "How Vast the Wasteland Now" speech from 1961. Does this question mean you find me frivolous? The truth is, I never forget that I am nothing more than a light in the box in the corner of the room and the viewer can switch me off. We have to recognize that the viewer has a very strong control over our lives: they have the "off" button and can easily turn over to other channels. So you have to keep them interested to make them want to tune in. We must remember that our duty is not only to inform and educate – but also to entertain. And sometimes we are going to cover frivolous stories but that is no difference from newspapers.

You have traveled around the US speaking to voters to previous elections. Are you going to do the same thing this election? Do you think that Bush's chance to win is not encouraging?

The Majesty of the Process. The People have spoken. The Polls have closed. What could be more magnificent to cover than an election – and I love them. It is a crucial moment when the people get their chance to speak and give their option about the governments that rule their lives. I very much hope I will be part of CNN's coverage of the 2008 US presidential election, since I have covered every US election for the past 20 years.

But with a predominantly pro-Bush Western press, do you think you get far?

I would disagree with the premise that the Western press is pro-Bush. If that was the case, why does the White House spend so much time criticizing the coverage? Why does the US Administration feel the media gives it such a hard time? You can't have your argument both ways!! In the UK, where I live, this is certainly not the case just look at the way the UK Government criticizes the BBC or the newspapers. And in the US Bush has his critics as much as he has his supporters. Election coverage is not about telling people who to vote for; it's about informing them of the issues so that they can make their democratic choice.

What frustrates you as a journalist?

The battle against time and resources. There are so many stories that I want to tell; but television is an extremely expensive business and there often isn't the time or money to get out and do it as I would wish. I am a part-idealist, so I always want more. But I am also a realist so I know the show has to be made, with the resources we have. And CNN is well resourced to tell the stories we need to tell. I am frustrated at media management both by companies and government. So many vested interests are now employed to get "a particular point of view" across that making sense of a story is a battled. Too many PR companies see it as their job to dictate the way a story goes, not merely to facilitate the journalist getting on with their job.

Who, according to you, is the toughest to interview?

There are so many different people who have been touch for different reasons. My object is always the same – to give the interviewee the chance to express themselves to the best of their ability. When I feel I am failing, I get very depressed.

Bill Clinton was hard, because he is such a clever man and I didn't want to get left behind. Archbishop Tutu was hard because I wanted to be precise in what we were talking about. Goldie Hawn was hard because she is a woman who is so engaging and yet we were talking serious matters of spirituality. Interviewing my mother was hard, because, well, she's my mother! She can always give me a clip around the ear and tell me to stop it!

What has hosting Business Traveller taught you?

As host of CNN Business Traveller, I have had the chance to travel all over the world reporting on a topic that I am passionate about. Research has shown that CNN viewers are frequent business travelers so it has been my privilege to be able to update them with the latest news in this sector and to develop my own knowledge of all the latest services available to make the life of the corporate traveler easier when on the road.

What would your advice be to promising journalists?

You need to care. Care about the facts. Care about telling a story. Care about getting it right. You need to care about the audience (they don't want to be hectored, lectured or bored). You need to care about yourself. Develop your own personal style and count yourself lucky to have joined this fabulous profession that enables us to witness the events that shape our world from the very frontline.

What is the future of space tourism in your opinion? Would you personally invest in such an experience?

Space tourism is never going to be cheap and will always remain in the domain of the elite. But it is going to become more widely available than the currently prohibitive $20 million price tag – which is what Anousheh Ansari paid for her recent trip to space. If Virgin Galactic succeeds, it is going to make it possible for us to experience the sense of leaving planet earth behind and looking down on it from space, even if only for a brief time. But it certainly won't make astronauts of us all.

What is your view on the future of cars twenty years from now and the impact it will have on people and the environment?

The main change we have seen in cars over the last twenty years – other than the ability to go at even faster speeds – have been improvements in their safety and their environmental impact. I see no reason why this trend won't continue and would very much expect that we will start to see cars that are not dependent on petrol and oil but will be using alternative, more environmentally-friendly means of power. But my job as moderator is not to let people know my views; it will be to find out the views of our highly-experienced panelists who are the experts in these topics.

Rashad Abu Shawar

Photo by Atef Awadat

Arabic novelist and rebellious storyteller Rashad Abu Shawer
'His is the voice that does not relax even on the Sabbath'

One of the most difficult tasks is to dwell deep into the cultural
life of the political writer. The Palestinian novelist and rebellious
storyteller Rashad Abu Shawer belongs to the creative, committed
genre of writers committed to write of their culture and literature,
unable to escape from the political idea that dwells in them, harking
back to the homeland and its dream. Abu Shawer who wrote
"Lovers" and "Crying on the chest of the beloved" is unswervingly

persistent in his writings. One critic said of him: His is the voice that does not relax even on the Sabbath.

Literary critics believe novelists project their own lives into their novels and write about their own experiences.
Abu Shawer is not exceptional in this.
Depending on a rich and detailed memory, Abu Shawer in his literary works, records his personal experiences as a Palestinian and his relationship with the Palestinian Revolution.
Born in 1942 in the village of Zakreen, Abu Shawer lived in refugee camps near Jericho until he joined the Palestinian revolutionary movement. With the fedayyeen, he moved from Amman to Damascus, Beirut and Tunis until he finally returned to Amman.
This story life left deep impressions on his creative work. "The relevance of my personal experiences to much of my works is very obvious," Abu Shawer said
Both the author and narrator in Shawer's novels represent their people warmly and intimately.
In 1973, Abu Shawer published 'Days of Love and Death' describing his life in his hometown Zakreen near Hebron during the period preceding 1948. The novel covers wide geographical territory and includes a large number of people so much so that it feels like a condensed summary of a great epic.
The Zakreen he presents is certainly not the Zakreen of today.
"Zakreen of the past was joyful, alive and proud. The Zakreen of today is intimidating, disfigured and broken," said the novelist. That is what Abu Shawer tried to show in his novel 'Days of Love and Death.'
One year after 'Days of Love and Death' he published 'Crying on a Lover's Bosom' telling the story of the 1970 confrontations in Amman between PLO guerrillas and the army.
In 1978, Abu Shawer recorded his experience as a little boy in the camp of Jericho in his novel 'Lovers.'

Abu Shawer' extensive preparatory work for his novels included collecting thousands of documents about the history of the setting of the events and of people.

"I don't depend only on my memory," he said. "What I remember about Palestine before the 1948 is only images so I search to produce the complete pictures of the past."

The novelist, however, believes that Palestine is not a "closed subject."

"Palestine is more than that — it is war, exile, fear, and martyrdom. Palestine is bravery, love and happiness," he said.

In 1982, he wrote about the PLO's inglorious exodus from Lebanon after the Israeli invasion of Beirut in a novel entitled "God did not Rest on the Seventh Day.' Abu Shawer said that Jews believe that God created the world in six days and rested on the seventh.

"The journey from Beirut to Tunis took six days, but we [Palestinians] did not rest in the seventh days because we started to prepare for another sacred resistance from Tunis," said the novelist.

Abu Shawer explained that in his 'God did not Rest on the Seventh Day,' he also meant to write about the real heroes of the conflict — the ordinary people of Lebanon and Palestine.

"Women, who used to prepare food for the guerrillas in the middle of the battle, are heroines. The boys who used to deliver the 'War' newspapers are also heroes," said Abu Shawer.

Abu Shawer's Zeinab's Windows' was published as a novel in 1994 and is about the first Palestinian uprising. It was Abu Shawer's first experience in writing novels and short stories was about Palestinian resistance and it was published as an article in 1967 in the Beirut-based 'Al Adab' magazine.

Following is extracts of an interview with Abu Shawer:

Is Rashad Abu Shawer, the writer, tiring after this long literary journey?

My stories and writings in local and Arab newspapers and my participation in seminars and celebrations suggest I am not tiring. Perhaps even my voice is more violent than in the past, for the Arab situation has worsened than ever before. We are at the nadir, the Arab man is violated, absent from all that is related to him and his future. Art, creativity, writing, and other literary forms stand in collision with everything that surrounds Arabs. My belief has always been clear and there is nothing that can change my mind and tires my convictions in my faith in Palestine and Arab unity.

What is the role of the writer at this stage and are you satisfied with his performance?

Many today have stopped talking about and/or writing of the unity of the Arab nation and are changing consciously or unconsciously into different beings, aided and abetted by a media communication system that espouses parochialism whilst in essence destroying the Arab nation and terrorizing all of its causes and leaving it in an underdeveloped state and obstructing its advancements.

You are a political writer, however, you write about love and sorrow. Is that a contradiction?

To be a human born in Palestine does not mean he should be closed-minded. If he encloses on himself, he would not serve the Palestinian cause and becomes parochial, only thinking of himself. I think about all of the issues of the [Arab] nation from

Yemen to Djibouti. Does this prevent me from writing stories about love? No, on the contrary, it does not. The most beautiful love stories are written in wars because they have intimate human moments …the need of women for men and the need of men for women, the human need to the house, children, for peace and assurance. All of these are missed in our lives. Moreover, if I miss them, more and more people long for them and desire them. So I write about them.

I do not write about the Palestinian cause from the angle of rifles, barrel of the gun or the moment of clash … All these occur within minutes or half an hour at most. The real clash is life in exile, alienation and harsh conditions that surround Palestinians and work to disappoint them as deliberate and intentional. So if we stop the first advancing trench and turn out the torch, darkness would prevail and the Zionist occupation will continue in its declared and undeclared forms.

Is it required that talent must be combined with awareness of the creative political writer?

Talent alone without culture and without affiliation is of no value. In the Arab world we all suffer, not necessarily as occupied peoples, as it is the case with Palestinians, we are occupied by underdevelopment, unemployment, poverty, hunger and all other kinds of malaise in the universe. What more than this does the writer need, he needs to be brave, honest, raise his voice, and enlighten people, not mislead them. There are intellectuals who play a misguided role. They lie and falsify. The one who depart from the main issues and never approaches them is a liar and misleader. He is concerned in forms and empty talk and writing becomes an escape from core issues. There are countries suffering unemployment, underdevelopment, and absence of law and freedom, and lack transparency. However, their writers are involved in talk about artistic forms of the poem, story and novel techniques.

Who is responsible for the cultural alienation that is taking place, what is the role of satellite channels in creating a simplified culture?

There is a so-called "culture of pettiness", I will not free those from the charge that they are trivializing entire Arab generations and keeping them away from the real issues, dwelling into peripheral subjects without culture and awareness. However, people will soon realize the pressures of reality and daily life when confronted with the lack of employment. Satellite TV will not solve the existing problems and will be shocked by the existing bureaucracies which disrupt their lives. This status quo reproduces consciousness whether we like it or not and my bet is on reality and on the Palestinian and Iraqi peoples.

As a novelist and creator, what does Land Day mean to you? Do you think Land Day has entered the arena of creativity and achieved what it was created for?

Land Day for the Palestinians is not 30th March 1976, but it is every day since the conflict began with the Zionist movement on the land. Every day in our life is a struggle on the ground; the land is for the Palestinian, the Palestinian himself, his presence and his being, it is the identity and meaning of his life. And when I say a Palestinian, I always warn this is not from a parochial point of view, but because it is the first line of defense against the Zionist Jews and of the Zionist Arabs!

War is not at an end, not even for a moment either by the enemy and/or by the spirit of the Palestinian people, whereas it is absent in the understanding of both the Palestinian and Arab leaderships. The Palestinian nation deserves a worthy leader like Abdul Qadir Husseini, who broke through all the villages. As an Arab writer, Land Day means to live day and night with the land and this is the role of each Palestinian writer and poet from Abdel Rahim Mahmoud, who was martyred on the soil of the tree that gave birth to Naji

Al-Ali and Ibrahim Touqan and all those giants who taught us. I can write a book about a bird in the sky, a dove and the tree for we are the sons of nature and the sons of these elements but I am also with Umm Nazim (mother of Nazim) who buries her three sons with dignity. Land Day means I am concerned; I am responsible for this land before the people and before the nation who own it.

These words are not mere narrative, every human on this earth has the right to a homeland, and the Palestinian land is the heart of the Arab world and the Palestinian is the guard of this heart and the soul and keeper of the whole nation.

If we look at the so-called peace process, we find it is they [Palestinian politicians] who assigned themselves as leaders of the Palestinian people, in reality, they stole the leadership and raped it; they went to Oslo and preached to the Palestinian people that peace is coming. When they announced they wanted to save the Palestinian land, I was in Tunisia and I opposed them strongly writing in Tunisian newspapers, with the Zionist enemy quickly resuming their acts and occupying more of the West Bank. Those who say they are fighting a battle for Jerusalem are misguiding the Palestinian people and Arab nation. There are no longer Jerusalem borders, as previously, the Adumim settlement creeps horizontally eastwards taking on the two sides and headed to the Khan Al-Ahmar overlooking Jericho and the Dead Sea. Land Day is a battle for the whole of Palestine, it is on a daily basis with its own mechanism, and should be breathed by true Palestinians, day and night.

How can Land Day be employed in works of great creativity to serve the cause of the Palestinian people on the human level and in the international relations arena?

Works on large scale need collective action, concerted actions, finance and those committed. It was tried by Palestinian musician

Hussein Nazik who lives in Syria, and who adapted the "Stranger and the Sultan" play to a kind of opera. We succeed when we write a poem, a novel and story but collective action is difficult, therefore, poems appeared on the ground and stayed with it, expressing it at home and abroad. One of the things achieved by Land Day since 1976 and after that made Palestinians realize, at home and abroad, they are one people and have one cause, and that Palestinians at home are the guardians of the land, giving them great pride and confidence.

I feel, man is born from birth to defend, to either cling to his right to stay or be forced out. The Zionist enemy wants to turn our people at home into beings without memory and without dignity.

The land cannot be liberated without heroism, martyrdom, challenges, blood and intelligibility. I heard someone say we are committed to the peace process! I say: Do it on your own! Israeli politicians say we will not halt settlement construction and expansion will continue, and you reply by saying we will continue our "peace offensive." Those have privileges that move and handicap them. They say the state of Palestine will have its capital Jerusalem, I ask: Can you remove the [Jewish] cities of Maalem, Chelom and Geeaa and others who love peace? These cities are "castles" lived in by tens of thousands of peoples, built and widened, and spread like cancer in the post-Oslo period. Those who bear responsibility should be put them on trial.

There are European civil institutions that stand against the Iraq war and the occupation of Palestine, they are asking us to send messages to send pictures expressing the pulse of the Arab street, and here I wonder what we shall send them. Shall we send pictures of traffic accidents and say these are caused by the terrible conditions of the streets!

Hada Sarhan

Why did you refused your works to be translated into Hebrew?

Emile Habibi called me one day and said, give me power of attorney to translate "Ah Ya Beirut" into Hebrew, I told him impossible. He then asked the poet Mohammed Hamza Ghanayem to translate "The Lord did not rest on the seventh day," I refused because it would have meant that there is communication with them [Israelis], and this means we have become friends. If they translated my works under the slogan of "know thy enemy" and I got to know of that, it does not matter. I know that some of them desperately sought to show they are for peace and relations of the two peoples…I'm not with the two peoples concept. I belong to one people who are part of one nation, there is no future on this earth, but for the Palestinian people.

This means you are against the hosting of people from "Israel" on the satellite channels.

Getting Israelis on these channels is a waste of time, these satellites are allowing the Jews to enter our homes and this should not be the case. We should not have to introduce their views through newspapers and dialogue with them, especially by those who believe Palestine is not for the Jews. As to those [Israelis] who say they are progressives and living in my house—I am supposed to negotiate with them? This is ridiculous.

After the 1948 catastrophe, you moved to Bethlehem and stayed in the Dheisheh Camp for four years, and become involved in the struggle that developed, tell us something about that life, culture of rebellion and Rashad Abu Shawer, one of the children of the stones at that time?

My family moved to the Dheisheh Camp in Hebron, I lived there until my 10th birthday. I remember we studied in tents, semi-naked, sitting on stones. One day I saw the adults in the camp shout for the right of return and as kids, we started to throw stones at the tents, a scene that remains in my mind, and from there began the relationship between the Palestinian people and the stones as if they were stoning the devil, world Zionism, Britain and others. My father was a communist and although he was illiterate, he had an open mind—and then we moved to the Nowhmieh Camp in the Jericho area. The Palestinians lived in camps on public roads as if waiting to return as quickly as possible. With this culture of spontaneity and automaticity, we lived in the camps, especially in Jericho and then my father moved us to Syria, to the Yarmouk Camp. There we learned the principles of return and love for Palestine and the responsibilities for return. It was clear from the outset that we will return and we have been ripped from our country, and Israel is our enemy, and without our unity, solidarity, determination, we will not be able to get our land back. When the late leader Jamal Abdel Nasser came on the scene, we began to be counted, especially as Sawt Al Arab (Voice of the Arabs radio station) started broadcasting, and of the many magazines, books and translations that filled our shops and stalls. These provided a source of information, education and culture. So this became the new groundings for a culture of belonging to the nation and we started to write Palestinian poems.

You wrote your novel, "Ah Ya Beirut" and threw yourself into the national struggle especially during 1982 and after. How do you feel about these years of woo in the light of what Lebanon is going through now?

Beirut is certainly dear to us, it always had a great cultural role, but Beirut's tragedy lies in its sectarians and loyalty to those outside Lebanon and outside of the Arab world.

You have dozens of publications. Are you satisfied with what you have written so far? What is new on the horizon?

I am not satisfied; sometimes I blame myself as I have a lot because of the experience I've been through. I need to extend my life 10 years more to be able to fill it with the serious works I have that contain Palestinian aspects, perhaps someone else will not be able to write about it. I do not mean I'm best technically, but of what I know and can be written down. I have accomplished much in the short story narrative and this is a something I feel pleased about. In the novel I have accomplished much as well but I have more.

Who have you been affected by in your writings? Are there schools of thought for literary novelists out there?

The novel is an open, limitless art, you can write about what you like. What is important is to convince and not to be contrived or false. I look at Ghasan Kanafani, Samira Azzam, and Jabra Ibrahim Jabra with respect. In poetry there are many, and there are also international writers like Dostoevsky and Hemingway whom I admire technically. The latter always impressed me by the simplicity and depth of his writings, in contrast to William Faulkner, who influenced Ghassan Kanafani's novels. There are many other writers we were affected by and loved and the experience of the generation that I am from, in reading and writing, is very wide.

What new offerings do you have?

The last collection of short stories, "Death Singing" is in its entirety about human oppression, humiliation, starvation, and being alien in the homeland. These are stories about unspecified place in the land of the Arabs.

Hans von Sponeck

Hans Christof Graf von Sponeck was born 1939 in Bremen, Germany,. He studied history, demography and physical anthropology in Germany and the USA and joined the UN Development Program in 1968,

Von Sponeck was awarded the 2000 Coventry Peace Prize by Coventry Cathedral and the 2000 Humanitarian Award from the American-Arab Anti-Discrimination Committee[7] and the 2003 Bremen Peace Award of the Threshold Foundation.

He served as a UN Humanitarian Coordinator for Iraq (1998-2000) and was appointed as the head of the UN World Food Programme in Iraq, but resigned in February 2000 to protest UN's Iraq sanctions policy. Von Sponeck accused the sanctions regime of violating the Geneva Conventions and other international laws and causing the death of thousands of Iraqis.

Your resignation on 2000 is very courageous. What makes you take such a strong protest action?

As the humanitarian coordinator at the time, I realized that the alleged concern for the welfare of the Iraqi people was nothing but a veil of pretention behind which major members of the UN Security Council planned their objective of regime replacement as a step towards consolidation of their power in the Middle East.

Some would say that to stay in office would help more the Iraqis?

Had I seen a chance to make a difference for the human condition in Iraq under the circumstances in which the UN Security Council found itself at the time, I would have been prepared to stay on. There was no such chance as the Security Council was thoroughly dominated by the US and the UK using as major weapons of influence false information on weapons of mass destruction as well as on the state of human suffering despite UN efforts in Iraq to report conditions as they existed on the ground in Iraq.

In your book "Iraqi Autopsy" you describe the dreadful situations of the Iraqi people mainly the children, why do you think the UN continues its policy of starvation of the innocent people of this country?

UN Security Council policy was heavily influenced by the US and the UK governments. This policy initially used economic pressure as a tool to obtain political change. When this failed to materialize they shifted their emphasis from containment to regime change without   concern for the people of Iraq. All 15 members of the Council were well aware of the evolving human catastrophe. The UN Security Council debates on Iraq give full testimony of this awareness. Most council members, however, did not have the political will let alone the moral integrity to make a difference against the heavy-handedness of the US and the UK governments and therefore share the burden of guilt.

Having served for thirty-six years with the UN organizations, what was your worst moment in your UN career?

I joined the UN in 1968 as a young international civil servant believing in the ideals of the Charta. Thirty years later, in Baghdad in 1998, I saw firsthand that the ideals and the rhetoric of statesmen in support of these ideals quickly gave way when it did not suit the political, economic and strategic interests of those in a position of power. The realization that commitment was really no more than hypocrisy, that an Iraqi life was worth much less than a barrel of Iraqi oil and that facts had no weight to influence policy and that all of this translated into total helplessness of an international civil service was my worst moment in the United Nations. It was this moment that made me decide to resign from an institution in which I believed.

Though it was proved that Iraq had fulfilled the disarmament requirements of resolution 687 which demanded of Iraq the disarmament of all of its weapons of mass destruction economic sanctions remained in place until the Anglo-American invasion of Iraq in March 2003.Economic sanctions remained in place until the illegal war of 2003 started because sanctions had little to do with freedom and liberation of a people. They had all to do with a determination to replace a dictator at whatever human cost for the sake of bilateral interests.

Do you agree that the positions taken by the United States in the Security Council during the 13 years of economic sanctions and military embargo against Iraq reveal that US Government concerns rested first with Iraq's weapons of mass destruction and US security interests?

It is a fact, not even hidden by the US government that US Iraq policy evolved much more around weapons of mass destruction and US security interests than the welfare of a people. On 7 April 2004, Ambassador John D. Negroponte in a briefing for the Committee on Foreign Relations of the US Senate made no secret out of this when he said: "Altough the flow of humanitarian and civilian goods to Iraq was a matter of strong interest to the US Government, it should be emphasized that an even greater preoccupation...was to ensure that no items were permitted for import which could in any way contribute to Iraq's WMD programs... We concentrated our efforts on this aspect of sanctions."

Why do you think despite the humanitarian programme socio-economic conditions in Iraq at the time sanctions were lifted in 2003 were so poor?

The humanitarian exemption for Iraq was at no time ever remotely adequate to meet the needs of the Iraqi people. The financial allocations were knowingly inadequate; the bureaucratic nature of the import of essential humanitarian goods was horrendous and avoidable. The result was that at the end of the oil-for-food prgramme at the time when the illegal invasion started in March 2003, the allocation of humanitarian supplies on which the vast majority of Iraqis had to rely amounted to an average of $ 186 per person per year. This was the amount individual Iraqis had for food, medicines, water, electricity and sanitation, agriculture and education. It is commonly accepted that a person with less than one dollar per day lives in abject poverty. Iraqis during 61/2 years of the oil-for-food programme were forced to live with less than half of this amount. It cannot surprise that this reality allows the conclusion that economic sanctions on Iraq constitute another crime against humanity.

Do you think that the Security Council acts for the benefit of the international community not in the interest of individual member states?

The UN Security Council has the responsibility to ensure that international policies are in the interest of the global community. Llyod Axworthy, Canada's foreign minister in the late 1990s reminded the Security Council of this responsibility when he said: "It is imperative that the sanctions reflect the objectives of the international community, not just the national interests of its most powerful members"! The Security Council was unable to prevent the United States government to convert the Council into a tool box to be used in the pursuit of narrow US policy interests.

Was the Security Council aware that the introduction of two no-fly zones in Iraq by the US, UK and French governments was without international mandate and therefore illegal?

The UN Security Council was fully aware that the southern and northern no-fly-zones originally established by the governments of the US, UK and France had no international legal basis and certainly no UN mandate. U.S and U.K references to various UN resolutions, particularly resolution 688, often used by the US and UK to justify the maintenance of the no-fly zones, did not provide in any way legal cover. The no-fly zones were simply illegal. The dishonesty of US and UK intentions became increasingly clear after the 1998 Operation Desert Fox when U.S and U.K pilots were given enlarged rules of engagement. This led to an increasing number of Iraqi civilian casualties as the UN reported from Baghdad in 1999/2000. For this the UN was reprimanded by the US and the UK and eventually forced to stop air strike reporting.

As the March 2003 date for the illegal US/UK invasion came closer, the two governments used the two no-fly zones to prepare for war by destroying military installations. The real objective of the maintenance of the two no fly-zones was not to protect ethnic and religious groups but in destabilizing the country.

Do you think that the reports sent by the investigators of mass destruct ions helped the US governments to invade Iraq?

The reports of UNMOVIC in late 2002/early 2003 were anything but helpful to the US as they showed that there were no traces of WMD as alleged by Secretary of State Colin Powell in his dishonest presentation to the UN Security Council on 5 February nor did Dr. Blix and his colleagues support the US contention that the Government of Iraq was uncooperative and therefore in 'material breach' justifying 'serious consequences' according to UN resolution 1441. The high costs of maintaining US and British troops in the Gulf, the deteriorating morale of the waiting troops, the soaring temperatures and an increasingly critical public back home and internationally combined with an unstoppable determination by the Bush administration to invade Iraq explain the start of the March 2003 war.

Was there any kind of corruption in the oil-for-food-program? And were there any "big" names involved?

The Third Volcker Commission report on the oil-for-food programme has just been issued and suggests that there has been individual wrongdoing. It is important to point out that there is no evidence that there is an institutional base of corruption but a limited though seriousmisuse of privileged position by a few.

Do you think there is a connection between invading Iraq and the worldwide spread of violence and terrorism?

As the recent Iraq Tribunal in Istanbul has shown, there is a world-wide anger against the US and the UK because of the illegal war against Iraq preceded by 13 years of devastating economic sanctions. This anger has unfortunately encouraged extreme elements to carry out acts of crime. A global public majority demands of political leaders that they address the causes of extremism as a first significant step towards reducing extremism and acts of crime. If leaders in the US and UK do not understand this demand they will continue to add to their liability for what must be expected as further deteriorating global security circumstances in the period ahead.

Stephen Farrell

Stephen Farrell is a journalist who holds both Irish and British citizenship and has been the Middle East correspondent for The Times. In July 2007, he joined The New York Times as a correspondent in Baghdad. He is married to Palestinian journalist Reem, and has just finished writing a book on Hamas. He has experienced kidnapping three times in his lifetime.

First he was kidnapped near the Iraqi city of Fallujah in 2004; he was set free after he managed to convince his captors that he was a genuine journalist Farrell said one had to tell the truth to save his life. In 2009, Farrell along with Sultan M. Munadi, an Afghan journalist working with him, was kidnapped by the Taliban in northern Afghanistan. Recently he was reported missing in the eastern Libyan town of Ajdabiya on March 2011, along with three other New York Times journalists. We met Farrell in Amman for an interview; following are some excerpts:

As Middle East Correspondent for The Times, is there any differences between the way Arab media and foreign media covers the same story?

Yes, but that is true in Britain, Ireland, Europe, India, and the Balkans, everywhere. Outsiders always see a region differently from insiders. Insiders always think foreigners are unfair to them. Outsiders always think insiders are biased toward their own country, city, religion, ethnic group political party or whatever. Insiders have more expert knowledge. Outsiders bring wider perspective from other wars, conflicts, peace processes. The Middle East is no different from anywhere else, except that people pay more attention to it.

What do you think as one who covers the Persian Gulf from Iraq and the on going Israeli-Palestinian conflict?

I think it is easier to understand the perspective of people from the region - on all sides - when you live and work here as a journalist than if you just arrive as a visitor for two or three weeks covering stories. However, after nearly six years in the Middle East I do not expect either conflict to be settled soon. In the Israeli-Palestinian situation there is so little trust on either side that I suspect no outside solution can be agreed in the present circumstances, and neither side seems capable of reaching an internally-agreed compromise. Iraq is grim, and likely to remain so for some time.

What events of yours were personal favorites and why?

Being in Baghdad on the day US troops arrived in the capital, and being in Firdos Square when the statue came down was probably the highlight of my career. Partly because it was such a huge story, partly because it had everything: release of emotions, the strength of the passions aroused, celebrations, shock, anger. Also because being there for a piece of history meant I could see everything that happened, rather than relying on other people's second-hand accounts, but mostly because while outsiders saw it as the end of something, on the ground it was obviously the beginning of something. All the seeds of what is happening now were there that day: Shia triumph, Baathist anger, Sunni uncertainty. The looting started immediately, and that was a very bad sign. Also, being in India for the Kumbh Mela Hindu religious festival just to see 20-30 million people in the same place.

Also being in Paris to cover the death of Diana, Princess of Wales, and being one of the only two reporters allowed into the hospital to talk to the doctors and staff of the hospital. The whole world was watching, and emotions were very high.

You were one of the first journalists kidnapped in Iraq in 2004. Would you tell us what happened during that ordeal.

I was driving from Amman to Baghdad in an armored car and this lorry came out of nowhere, with about 20 people with Kalashnikovs and rocket propelled grenade launchers and started spraying Kalashnikov bullets at the car. I did a U-turn and headed off in the other direction, but they shot out my tyres and grabbed us out of the car 10 seconds and led us off to a safe house. As I got out of the car, there was a guy who grabbed me by the throat and my watch was away within a second or two. At first I thought looting. Hands were going through my pockets. They took everything, $15,000 cash, and identity cards. They were scouring my passport screaming "Britani, Britani!" I actually have an Irish passport and a British passport, but they got the British one first. Then my colleague was American, which didn't help. And as we were driven away in a taxi, one guy was trying to blindfold me while head butting me at the same time. The guy on my right had a knife to my throat. The guy in front of me had a Kalashnikov to my head, they then handed us over to these guys knowing that they could get brownie points, if you like, from the bigger fish, the insurgents, for handing over somebody who could prove a value political kidnap tool. The second group.. Resistance – the guerrillas, insurgents, whatever you want to call them – just happened to stumble on us or their own intelligence network had picked up and they came to get us. They interrogated us more much more calmly, but much more professionally, for the best part of eight hours. The same questions, again and again and again, Arabic, English, Arabic, English, until finally they satisfied themselves that they were journalists.

We thought we'd been grabbed by a butch of bandits who led us to a safe house. As we were led into that, the

They've got access to Google. They check you out very, very quickly. They knew who I was within half a second of opening a car door and dragging us out.: I and I work in Baghdad

I had one already, it was the truth. And I decided that's what you're going to do. There's no point in hiding the fact that you've come from Jerusalem, for various long paper chain reasons. They'd either find out you were keeping quiet where you were coming from, or they'd find the document that showed where you were.

If you're flat out open with it and say, "I am a Middle East correspondent, so what? How do you expect me to cover the siege of Jenin, how do you expect me to cover the death of the Hamas leader Sheikh Yassin if I'm not in Jerusalem moving through to Gaza and the West Bank?"

Some accuse foreign reporters of not being objective in covering stories mainly about Arab war?

Many foreigners think people from this region are not objective, that they take sides based on their political, religious or national views. And when war is concerned, people are inevitably colored by their fears and the fears of their society. Many people - westerners and Arabs - are very scared at the moment, and this probably reduces objectivity.

What do you believe journalism is?

Journalism, for me as a correspondent, is the attempt to describe the reality of a situation and to accurately reflect the lives, opinions and perspectives of the people - powerful and ordinary alike. The truth is sometimes not what it appears to people in the country you report on, and sometimes not what it appears to people in your own country.

-Do you get involved in your coverage? And how does scene of victims affects your?

I try not to get involved. Obviously human pain and distress does affect anyone, but a journalist who gets carried away with emotion when surrounded by other people's suffering is about as useful as a surgeon who faints at the sight of blood.

Larry E. Park

A Vietnam Army medic who cared for some of the most severely injured men, women, children and babies from both sides of that conflict in 1970 and 71, Larry E. Park, understand the catastrophic toll in the present and the impact it will have on future generations.

He wrote his "apology" to the Iraqi people in which he writes: I feel shame and outrage when I watch on TV and read reports of unimaginable acts against humanity in Iraq. You are witnessing these horrific acts of violence and human debasement up close, which is probably filling your heart with hate and anger towards Americans. I'm sorry and I understand.

We met Larry Park through the world of internet and asked him why you wrote the "Apology?" he said:

- I felt powerless to change American public opinion concerning the US military occupation in Iraq, which in my view was waged under the guise of revenge for the 911 attacks. And then when Senator John Kerry lost the 2004 Presidential election, hope for a major policy shift in the White House was crushed. In my despair, I challenged God. "What can I do?" I asked Him. "Write an apology to the Iraqi people" was His answer. He inspired me to apologize. I wrote the "Apology to the Iraqi people" as a means of acknowledging that a wrong had been knowingly committed against real men, women and children and to sincerely attempt to convey a deep sense of sadness and remorse concerning the destruction of their infrastructure, injuries and loss of life within families. I feel shame that I did not raise my voice in dissent prior to this horrific conflict between cultures. I survived Vietnam with full understanding of what a guerilla war means and the futility of large, noisy, highly visible armies attempting to subjugate citizens by force instead of winning hearts and minds over to a more positive pursuit of happiness. I apologize for our arrogance in thinking we knew what the best course of social/political direction for Iraq was—and then we intervened militarily in such a destabilizing and catastrophic manner. Freedom is not a gift; it is a choice requiring daily action to reaffirm long-term goals and guide one in the pursuit of happiness. Your people are in the midst of personal and national conflict revolving around differences in opinion on how to equitably achieve goals within the context of your many subcultures. Intervention by outsiders has made the process more complex. I apologize! I carried a typewriter to Vietnam—not a gun—and instead of killing humans, I planted flowers and was awarded a Bronze Star medal for extending hope to others.

Do you think that America is more secure after its war on Afghanistan and invasion of Iraq?

My response to your questions might give you a different slant on these very important concepts of: firstly, a personal sense of safety, secondly, impact of 911 on global relations and thirdly, the role of government in gaining support for war on foreign soil. First, let me define security as a perception of being able to safely participate in daily activities of living within the social context of family, community and having the freedom to interact within the geographic boundaries of a sovereign nation for economic activity or the pursuit of happiness.

I believe the war in Afghanistan was a revengeful act against Taliban leaders that had overtly or covertly supported Osama Bin Laden's base of operations. The conflict between this former educated trainee of the CIA, Bin Laden, and America found its roots when he saw our hearts close up and was sickened by the preponderance of greedy control we exercised in Mid Eastern countries for our own profit and to secure access to natural resources. I do not condone his acts of violence, I do attempt to understand his frustration, but his effort to persuade large numbers of peoples all over the planet to rise up against the United States cannot be stymied by brute military strength and deployment. Osama Bin Laden finds his voice in the wilderness by representing hordes of economically suppressed humans. America's multinational corporations are focused on profit, not their abuse of cheap foreign labor so we have a hard time selling America the rhetorically beautiful to those oppressed.

The infamous 911 call made by a disgruntled former employee of America's Central Intelligence Agency blew the whistle on America's long history of hegemony and was a call for emergency attention to past and present Arab grievances. A retired American General responded astutely to the call just days afterwards with his recommendations; "Unless the gross inequities between the haves and have-nots are addressed, terrorism will continue to flourish." Global terrorist leaders do not have recruiting problems during this pivotal time in earth's history.

Unfortunately the American 911 dispatcher put the caller on hold while sending shock, awe and armies of ground troops to attack the vulnerable and impoverished seeking relief from tyranny and deprivation. Like New Orleans , a global human emergency calling for positive remedial action turned into a disaster by the wrong response.

The call was made for help, but due to a lack of understanding and our leader's vision clouded by dreams of a One World government, America weighed in the balance of blind justice has come up short.

America's sense of invulnerability was stripped away when the haughty, towering symbols of her economic strength turned to dust and her citizens realized that their rhetorical plea, "God Bless America" so often pronounced to lull them to sleep was not being heard in the courts of Heaven because she had ignored the cries of the oppressed.

No, America is not more secure because of the invasions of Afghanistan and Iraq. The conflict lies within our hearts as we daily are confronted with the specter of human need near and afar. That conflict becomes visible when we chose to actively uplift the impoverished of spirit and equip them to be productive instead of doing nothing by the default of a self serving mind set or exploiting their weakness in acts of racial genocide.

How would you evaluate American foreign policy after September 11?

— I must first establish a standard of reference by which individual and corporate conduct is measured: I do not claim to have the experience nor the ability to evaluate the pros and cons of American foreign policies overt and covert in all instances because my feeble analysis might fall short of any rational understanding and probably would end up as spin exploited, opposing my perspective. One is compelled to search for a standard of perfection that guides imperfect humans on their path of long term interdependent relationships and the pursuit of happiness. I make no apologies in identifying my standard by which all nations are weighted, the one and only Creator God who made the planets, stars and all the creatures and plants found on our shared home, know as earth. President George W. Bush in the aftermath of 911 identified the message of the urgent call to all mankind well, when he posed the rhetorical challenge "Are we going to live in freedom or in fear?" I was awestruck by his comment that echoed my personal perceptions of the original insurgent rebellion in Heaven as interpreted by the theologians of Judeo Christian origin. Does our Creator God rule as a despot forcing us to obey Him like preprogrammed robots or are we free agents to chose loyalty to Him or follow the lies of the original mastermind of terror, Lucifer the aberrant choirmaster who commandeered one third of the universe's administrators called angels? Bush went on to say that the world must choose sides. Those countries who choose to follow or support Osama Bin Laden were forced into the corner of decision and their very lives and economic futures depended on whether or not they stood behind Bin Laden or grabbed onto the outstretched hands of American hegemony.
President Bush got the message about core issues between good and evil, but his methods to confront evil at home and abroad were ill conceived to win the war on original terror.

Depending on where one lived on the planet probably contributed significantly to whether or not individuals identified Bush as the Devil or Osama Bin Laden as the evil one. Men and nations have become the pawns of the original Prince of Darkness, Lucifer identified in the book called the Bible. Only God can ultimately judge who is good or evil and "Vengeance is mine" he said as recorded in the book held high by America.

The representative government of America made themselves into gods and decided to whom and where they would mete out vengeance. God doesn't like imposters and He warned that those who kill by the sword, die by the sword. Flag draped coffins returning to the shores of America attest to this principle as insurgents also meet their maker in judgment.

We have all witnessed evil deeds done by all sides of this quagmire of war in Iraq and Afghanistan and many trees claiming to bear freedom's fruit have only born rotten apples. Using God's laws of mercy, forgiveness and the implementation of the "Golden Rule" of doing onto others as you would like it done onto to you seems foreign to many who give advice to the President of the United States of America.

Well, Hada you could take the position that America's god has been killed by science, Islam's Creator known as Allah is just a hyped up monotheistic moon god and the supernatural being many religions call the devil is just the wild imaginations of men exploiting the concept of good and evil for their own covert actions. America's greatness was born out of tolerance for a difference of opinion and the freedom to believe or not believe in supernatural forces good or evil. Many of Europe's inhabitants fled to America, avoiding burnings at the stake and rolling of heads at the hands of religious zealots. The issue of: Is there a god? What kind of god is he? She or it and who's side is he on echoes the past, but has to be addressed again in the present as nations claim superiority based on rhetorical religious pronouncements and deluded convictions that their god is blessing them in whatever they do or don't do.

The trees of "freedom" are judged by the kind of fruit they bear. That axiom stands whether or not one believes in a Creator God. America's self-centered successful foreign policies of the past 85 years related to access to global natural resources, abuse of the marketplace to economically enslave impoverished peoples all over the planet to produce cheap goods and recent borrowing practices from other nations has emboldened its leaders instead of humbling them in the light of 911 grievances. President George W. Bush and his advisors just don't seem to understand why many of the other developed and underdeveloped countries perceive America as the oppressor and stumbling block for the rest of mankind on a path to uncontrolled decadence. America's pagan culture in the guise of false religion is being unmasked and her fruit has spoiled the world. Those who follow her example will inherit the broken society she sells so boldly and if the American soldiers that have set foot on foreign soil are the representatives, ambassadors of good will, then our foreign policy is in a shambles. The Iraqi people have seen our hearts and their hopes for peace on earth and good will to all men have been destroyed by the evil unmasked during times of war. It appears that America's present foreign policy will lead to the partial or complete destruction of almost every city large or small in Iraq before our destroying presence is withdrawn.

One of the largest Tsunamis in recorded history gave Bush the political opportunity to save face, withdrawal troops to assist with disaster relief, rebuilding, shore up Asian relationships and build trust with people of the Islam faith, but he ignored the call. Katrina 911 again on a domestic level offers him a gilded opportunity to save face, begin a progressive withdrawal of troops from Iraq and Afghanistan and reassign them to missions of mercy and rebuilding.

America's foreign policy will only be deemed a success when unarmed American citizens as tourists, aide workers, temporary contractors and or residents can live and travel throughout Iraq and Afghanistan without fear of death. When in the next 40 years, over the life of the oil lease agreements between American multinational oil companies and those who control the reserves might that happen? Peace and good will are going to be harder to find then new deposits of black gold on the planet.

Individual and global conflict turned ugly is a symptom of human spirits controlled by evil forces manmade or supernatural depending on your core beliefs. Those who attempt to promote peace and harmony among humans are constantly assailed by forces that are hell bent on destroying the planet and its inhabitants. From God's perspective it sure looks like planetary suicide and that behavior is exemplified in America's manufacture and use of radioactive depleted uranium munitions and armor.

In summary Hada, the visible fruits of American foreign policy are often counter productive and military actions in Iraq and Afghanistan sets an example of governmental lawlessness, called anarchy.

Do you believe that the Bush Administration used misinformation to persuade Americans to be complacent about invading and occupying Iraq ?

- I had watched Tariq Aziz many times during diplomatic negotiations involving teams of UN inspectors and during the buildup and invasion of Iraq . He seemed credible, conveyed diplomatic skill, confidence and I believed him when he dismissed the accusations from America's State Department that Iraq had WMD. I have heard that he might be released soon and hope he can join his family in Amman. The bottom line for me personally is: war often separates family members temporarily or in death permanently unless you are a Christian like Tariq Aziz who claims to believe in the resurrection of life eternal for those who believe in their savior Jesus Christ. Separation from those you hold in high esteem and love is the ultimate human tragedy!

Like many Americans, I hoped that all the posturing and rattling of sabers was going to resolve differences between Saddam Hussein and America through diplomatic means while many seemed to relish the idea of a destructive shock and awe attack on Baghdad.

We all make individual choices whether or not to believe in concepts promoted by politicians, preachers of faith and we even attempt to filter the advice coming from our spouse or best friend. Sometimes we don't even form an opinion because the issue is of no apparent importance to us personally and or we don't think that one engaged citizen can make a difference on the global stage of negative or positive interdependent relationships.

I came down off the fence of indecision onto the anti-war side when I discovered the government denial and the collaborating media cover up concerning the damage to humans, plants and animals related to toxic depleted uranium munitions used in Iraq and Afghanistan. We are killing the planet and it inhabitants.

I like to think that I am more than just another deluded American, who thinks he can make a meaningful difference in the global process of informing this generation about the long term hazards of radioactive nuclear waste.

Cars, houses and luxury yachts do not fulfill the true American Dream. Men just wanted a voice to dispel the darkness of corruption and control by despot religious leaders of millennia past. The original founding fathers gave us the freedom of speech, the promise to be allowed to pursue happiness and exercise freedom of conscience.

An international ban on the manufacture, use of depleted uranium in munitions and armor and the destruction of stockpiled weapons would be a first step on the journey of destroying all weapons that have the potential of planetary annihilation. Obviously any country that has nuclear waste has the potential of manufacturing WMD and or using that waste to contaminate the environment for purposes of genocide. Misinformation and infrequent media attention to this issue of great importance continues. Mothers on both sides of this conflict will figure out the relationship between DU and birth defects, rise up and lead the fight against the warmongers.

Tell us more about your book "Stimulus N Flashbacks 30 Years Searching for Balance"?

The title is an adaptation of psychological behavioral testing where subjects are "stimulated" and then the "response" is recorded. If one Google "flashbacks" one will find research related to how a very traumatic experience like war or rape can be relived months or years later when a stimulus in the present triggers a total recall of that painful memory of a past event.

Each chapter in my book represented a flashback generated by a specific issue in the present and even though Abu Ghraib became public after I had written about atrocities, I knew that in any war they are perpetrated. My book was a warning about the untold consequences of war.

Ben Wedeman

CNN's Cairo bureau chief Ben Wedeman has lived in the Middle East since 1974, during which he worked as a freelance at "The Star" his second home as he described it.

Fluent in Arabic, Italian and French, Wedeman has received numerous awards for his work, including a 2000 Emmy Award for Outstanding Coverage of a Continuing News Story/Segments and a 2000 Edward R. Murrow Award for coverage of the war.

You worked as a freelance print journalist in "The Star", for two years how do you evaluate that period?

- The Star's offices in Amman's Jebel Leweibda quickly became my second home in the Jordanian capital when I moved there in September 1993. Thanks to Editor-in-chief Osama Sherif, managing editor Marwan Al-Asmar and chief reporter Ra'id Abid, I quickly learned the ins and outs of Amman. They helped me develop my contacts, which later proved invaluable when I started working with CNN the following year. The Star was my base for getting to know Jordan, and it was there that I became the front page editor. Osama also gave me the green light to begin my weekly column, Press Cocktail, where I would review the more interesting and quirky articles in the Jordanian press which, at the time, was really beginning to flourish as the late King Hussein oversaw a democratic opening long before democracy in the Arab world became all the rage. And it was for the star that I covered the Jordanian parliamentary elections in November 1993. I had moved to Jordan from Syria, where I had seen one sham election after another, and therefore I thoroughly enjoyed and relished the parliamentary vote in Jordan where I could see a much freer, more open and genuine exercise in democracy. The staff of the Star was passionate about the news, and nothing would be more welcome there than a great story to cover. And it was a time when much was happening. I moved to Amman just days after the Oslo accords were signed, and Jordan was abuzz with talk of what peace would mean. It was a time of optimism, when people— politicians, journalist and ordinary Jordanians—could, for the first time in years, ponder the possibilities. Tourism, economic development, the repercussions of a new era, were very much the focus of many of our always animated conversations. And never was the Star more animated than on Thursday evenings, when the paper went to the printer at the headquarters of Al-Addustour, Amman's premier Arabic daily. Thursday evenings were always manic events, as we rushed to get the paper out, under the always demanding eye of editor Marwan, who would mix laughs with curses to make sure we made our deadline. Working with the

Star, I didn't make much money (who did?), but it was probably the funniest job I ever had.

What are your aims and objectives?

- My aim as a journalist working for CNN in the Middle East is to give our international audience insights into what drives this important region-politically, socially and economically. I do this by not only speaking with the region's leaders, experts and analysts, but also by speaking with ordinary people who are impacted by change, and often pay the highest price for policies and decisions made thousands of kilometres away. I always try to get the opinion of those whose voices are sometimes ignored or neglected.

For example, after the recent bombings in Dahab, I interviewed not only Egyptian Prime Minister Ahmed Nazif, but also the inhabitants of Dahab—shopkeepers, workers and others. Later, I travelled to Al-Arish, the home of many of the people accused of involvement in the Sinai attacks, and interviewed relatives of some of the suspects as well as human rights activists there. I try to cover every angle of the stories I cover.

I believe it is critical that we as journalists go beyond the obvious, avoid stereotypes and show our audience this is a diverse region where there is no uniformity of opinion. Another of my objectives is also to make sure my reporting is first-hand. As a correspondent I want to be where things happen, not get the footage from others and base my reporting on second-hand accounts. I don't like to work through producers and translators. I want to hear directly what people are saying and draw my own journalistic conclusions.

What have been your career highlights?

- One of the stories that really stand out, due to the journalistic challenges it presented, was the collapse of the Israeli-Palestinian peace process. Beginning in Jordan in 1993, I covered the initial euphoria that followed the signing of the Oslo Peace accords, followed in 1994 by the Wadi Araba agreement between Jordan and Israel. Hopes were so high on both sides of the conflict that a new era was beginning. But I also listened very closely to the critics of the peace process. I would often visit my friends at Al-Sabil newspaper in Amman, who provided me with useful insights into the shortcomings of the American-sponsored peace process and eloquently explained to me the Islamist critique of the process. I was a witness to the gradual crisis of the high hopes of the peace process, in Israel, the West Band and Gaza, in Jordan and in Lebanon.

I was in Israel, the West Bank and Gaza in the summer of 2000, while Yasser Arafat, Ehud Barak and Bill Clinton were trying to make progress in Camp David. I realized at the time, after speaking with dozens of Israelis and Palestinians, that the peace process was in a profound crisis, and that an explosion was coming. And they were right. In September 2000, the second intifada broke out, and since then hopes for peace have faded steadily.

I am also proud of my years of coverage of Iraq. I first went to Baghdad in 1994, and went there regularly until June 2004. I always enjoyed getting to know Iraqis—a wonderful people cursed by recent history.

What events of yours were personal favorites and why?

The story that meant the most to me was the civil war in Sierra Leone in May 2000. Going to the front lines almost every day, I was able to cover the insanity of a conflict that was mind bogglingly brutal, where the different factions would amputate arms, legs, ears and noses of innocent civilians. It was a difficult story to cover and I suffered from nightmares for months afterwards, but as journalists we encountered none of the limitations that sometimes make work in the Middle East so difficult. No one ever said no, no one ever said "mamnoua'a". No other network covered the story like CNN, and we received two awards, an Emmy and a Murrow, for our coverage of this story. I think our coverage alerted people outside Sierra Leone, especially in the United States, that this was conflict humanity could not allow to go on.

What do you see as the main reasons for your consistent success in the business?

- I don't know if I can say I have had consistent success. Like every journalist, I have had my ups and downs. But I think the most important element for success as a journalist is to always care about the stories you cover. To have empathy for the people you cover. To understand, though not necessary agree with, the motives of the people you cover.

*Being CNN's Cairo bureau chief is there any differences between the way Arab media and foreign media covers the same story?

- I don't really like to generalize about the Arab media, since it is so diverse. Obviously the Arab media is addressing an Arab audience, which tends to be much more familiar with the details of the stories in the region, whereas the foreign media has to provide much more historical, political or social context for an audience that is not as well-informed about the region. Sometimes the Arab media intensely covers stories that, to a non-Arab audience might not seem so important. It is our task to sort things out and determine what is important to an audience whose attention is not so wholly focused on this region.

Having a bachelor's degree in Arabic how would this help you in your work?

- I have been speaking Arabic since my early teens, when I lived in Beirut. Speaking Arabic, I have been able to hear first hand what people think and feel, without having to work through translators. And speaking Arabic (or any other language) you pick up so much more than just the words. I am able to directly tap into the depth of emotion that is behind the words people speak, I am able to pick up on historical, religious and social references that others who don't speak Arabic would never understand. In short, speaking Arabic has been critical to my success as a journalist. In fact, I think it is critical that we as international journalists do our best to learn whatever language the people around us speak. In 2000, when I covered a famine in the Somali-speaking area of Ethiopia, I did my best to learn a bit of Somali. When I covered the war in Afghanistan in 2001, I tried to learn Dari, the dialect of Farsi spoken in the northern part of the country and in Kabul. I have been studying Hebrew since I began covering Israel as well. I believe any journalist who doesn't understand at least some of the language people around him are speaking is not doing their job.

Some accuse foreigner reporter that they are not objective in covering stories mainly about Arab war? What do you think as a one who covers the Persian Gulf from Iraq and the ongoing Israeli-Palestinian conflict?

I can't speak for others, but for my part, I do my utmost to make sure my reporting is objective. I have never shied away from showing all sides of the conflicts I cover. In Iraq, I covered stories like the Abu Ghraib torture scandal and US military operations that shocked me with their brutality and insensitivity. I have been criticized by all sides in many of the conflicts I have covered, and I am proud of that criticism as a sign that I am being fair. My philosophy is to question the claims by all sides, regardless of who is making them.

About the Author

Hada Sarhan started writing about cultural issues when she was a student at Yarmouk University, where she graduated with a major in English Language. Her exposure to English and American literature enriched her writings.

Throughout her career, she has also assisted international media as an interpreter and as a reporter such as the London Times, Stern and others. She was nominated by the London-based Production Company for the best free lance of the 2010 for her works as a consultant, translator and researcher in international rewarded documentary films titled Serjio, on the explosion of the UN offices in Baghdad and Jihad: The Men and Ideas Behind Al-Qaeda.

Currently she is a Columnist and Head of the Cultural and International News Department at Al Arab AlYawm Daily newspaper, Before that, she was the culture reporter at the Jordan Times, the country's only English daily newspaper.

Hada has two books in Arabic: "Reem asks: Who am I?" and "When Men Flee" in addition to a book in English titled "Women Say NO"

Hada Sarhan is a member at: The Jordanian Press Syndicate, Arab Women's Media Centre and Jordanian Writers Association

Appendices

Abdel Bari Atwan: born in 1950 in Deir el-Balah, a Palestinian refugee camp in the Gaza Strip. He was one of 11 children. After receiving his primary school education at the camp, his schooling was continued first in Jordan in 1967, and then in Cairo, Egypt.

In 1970 he entered Cairo University where he studied journalism and also received a diploma in English-Arabic translation. In 1978, he moved to London, where he has lived ever since,

In 1989, al-Quds al-Arabi was founded by expatriate Palestinians and Abd al-Bari Atwan was offered the job as editor-in-chief, which he has held since. The paper has as of 2007 grown into one of the major pan-Arab dailies, and is known for its strident Arab nationalism and defense of the Palestinian cause. He has written two books: *The Secret History of Al-Qa'ida*, and *A Country of Word*.

Ahmad Al-Shuqairi : the first Chairman of the Palestine Liberation Organization, serving in 1964–67.

Amjad Nasser: prominent Jordanian poet, he lives in London, head of the cultural department at Alquds Al Arabi

Fedayyeen: refers to militants or guerrillas of a nationalist orientation from among the Palestinian people. Most Palestinians consider the fedayeen to be "freedom fighters",[

Fateh Movement is a major Palestinian political party and the largest faction of the Palestine Liberation Organization (PLO), a multi-party confederation.

Ghasan Kanafani, was a Palestinian writer and a leading member of the Popular Front for the Liberation of Palestine He was assassinated by car bomb in Beirut in July 8, 1972 in Beirut, Lebanon.

Hanafi Islamic school: is one of the four Madhhab (schools of law) in jurisprudence (Fiqh) within Sunni Islam, the other three schools of thought being Shafi'i, Maliki, and Hanbali. The Hanafi madhhab is named after the Iraqi scholar Abu Hanifa an-Nu'man

Jabra Ibrahim Jabra: was a Palestinian Poet, novelist, translate and literary critic of Syrian-Orthodox origin he settled in Iraq following the events of 1948. He has also translated some English works into Arabic

Jamal Al Shalabi: Researcher and professor in political science at the Hashemite University in Jordan. **Jamal Al Shalabi:** is an associate professor in the International Relations and Strategic Studies Program at the Hashemite University in jordan. He holds a doctorate degree in political science from the Faculty of Law, University Panthéon-Assas (Paris 2) in 1995, and he is an Award-Winning of the Arab Culture Award from UNESCO in 2006. He has many translations and publications that deal with the Arab-European relations and the civilization dialogue.

Jibril Rjoub a former security head who is a member of the central committee of the mainstream Fatah Organization

Khaled Mhadin, Jordanian writer and politician
Fares Nabulsi, **former Minister of Justice and a former PM**

Mahmoud Darwish, renowned Palestinian poet

Mamdouh Abbadi, Jordanian doctor and a PM

Mohamed Dahlan: a Palestinian politician, the former leader of Fatah in Gaza.

Mahmoud Al-Kayed was former *editor*-in-*chief* of Alrai newspaper/ Jordan

Nashed Ikhwan: traditional sweet was well-known in the sixties

Naji Al-Ali was a Palestinian cartoonist, noted for the political criticism of Israel in his works. he was shot in the face and mortally wounded.[3] Naji al-Ali died five

Samira Azzam, Palestinian short stories writer, died at a young age due to complications of the heart once she learned of the fall of Jerusalem in June 1967.

Wahhabi school: is a religious movement or a branch within Sunni Islam It was developed by an 18th century Muslim theologian (Muhammad ibn Abd al-Wahhab) from Najd, Saudi Arabia, who advocated purging Islam of "impurities".

Wahhabism is the dominant form of Islam in Saudi Arabia. It has developed considerable influence in the Muslim world in part through Saudi funding of mosques, schools and social programs.